Modular Crochet

A Revolutionary New Method for Creating Custom-Design Pullovers

by Judith Copeland

M. Evans and Company, Inc.
New York, New York 10017

Library of Congress Cataloging in Publication Data

Copeland, Judith.
  Modular crochet.

  1. Crocheting. 2. Sweaters. I. Title.
TT825.C66   746.9'2   78-3704
ISBN 0-87131-256-5

Manufactured in the United States of America.

9 8 7 6 5 4 3 2 1

To my mother,
who taught me the value of independent thinking

Photography: Andrea Blanch

Illustrations: Carol Hines

Hair Styling: Louis Alonzo

I would like to thank my husband Robert Copeland for his editorial guidance; Marga Bremer, Glen Burnside, Millie Garcia, Chin Hsin Chen, Pak Nang Lau, Esther Rosenstark, and Fumi Wellington for taking great care with the pull-overs they crocheted; Terry Arthur, Glen Burnside, Diana Cecil, Taylor Drotman, Cindy and Seth Greenberg, Constance Kevlock, Michael Levy, Kim Neblett, and Dana Nicholson for contributing their time and enthusiasm in the modeling of the garments. And finally, I would like to express my appreciation to the people at M. Evans and my many professional friends for their freely given advice and support as this book was being put together.

Contents

Introduction

Modular Crochet is an exciting new method for making crocheted garments. It has been developed for people who would like to design their own pullovers but need a way of working that will help them understand the structure of a garment and how to assemble its various parts. In evolving the modular way of working we have done two things that make the task of working on your own easy and efficient. First, we have considered the garment to be composed of rectangles—one of the most elementary forms—and have joined these rectangles together as simply as possible. Second, we have done away with the usual figures and computing that confuse so many crocheters and teach you instead through photographs and diagrams how to make garments by working directly on the body. To sum up quickly, this is how Modular Crochet works: You work the garment vertically from a beginning center chain that is made to fit right to your body. The length of the chain depends on your size and the style of the garment. You then add the rectangles one at a time, on each side of the chain, by working right onto the existing pieces; and you also fit them right to your body. Because you are working vertically and from the center of the body out, you can try on the garment to check your progress every step of the way. This makes it extraordinarily easy to get a good custom fit—the main problem most people encounter when crocheting a garment. In Modular Crochet, since all garments in all styles are made from six or eight rectangles, which are joined together in the same way, you do not need the usual written instructions for each individual project. You can achieve tremendous variation in styling and silhouettes by making the rectangles different sizes or varying your choice of yarn, color, and stitch. The results are all kinds of pullovers that are quick and easy to make. Even the most timid crocheters will find the method simple. It is, of course, a perfect way to introduce beginners to the art of crocheting, for they can turn out a sophisticated garment on their first try. To work in the modular method all you need to know are:

a. How to make the chain stitch

b. How to make the three basic stitches: the single crochet, the half double crochet, and the double crochet

c. How to crochet back and forth in a straight line

To teach you how to work in the modular way there are five lessons with easy-to-follow, step-by-step photographs, diagrams, and explanations which tell you what to do in plain sentences, avoiding, whenever possible, the usual crochet abbreviations: *Lesson 1* shows how all rectangles are joined for all garments. *Lesson 2* shows how to alter rectangles 1 through 4 for the different neck styles. *Lesson 3* tells how to read and use the diagrams. *Lesson 4* tells how to work from the photographs and the diagrams so that you can duplicate the styles shown in the size you want. Also each project is based on a different theme to illustrate some of the ways in which the modular pullover can be modified for different effects and styles. *Lesson 5* tells how to design and work on your own, and by the time you are done with this lesson you should be able to select any yarn and make a pullover in any size and style you wish.

About Stitches and Detailing tells you how to make the three ridge stitches, how to sew up seams, and how to work sleeves in the round. These fine points and other techniques described are of particular interest since good detailing is especially important in simple garments. *About Yarn* discusses the characteristics of the various fibers used and lists them in an easy referral chart. If you want to see how the yarns look made up consult the color photographs. You will note that the modular pullover can be transformed into a completely different garment simply by using a different yarn; each yarn creates a fabric that looks and behaves in its own special way. Garments made from rectangles can be as simple or as dramatic as you wish. For instance, the plain, unadorned rectangles, worked in the same yarn throughout and in neutral colors, make garments that are practical, comfortable, and easy to wear. The highly decorative rectangles, worked in a variety of yarns, colors, and stitches, or crocheted in a highly textured yarn such as a bouclé, make fanciful vests, fringe-covered ponchos, and handsome turtlenecks. Rectangles tapered at one end, by combining short and long stitches in the same row, make more complex or shaped garments, such as the bloused and smocked silhouettes. These are just a few of the possibilities inherent in the modular approach; there are as many variations as there are crocheters. This way of working means simple shapes and simple construction, with easy-to-learn and easy-to-apply techniques. In essence, Modular Crochet has made two key decisions for you—the shapes of the individual pieces and how they are put together. The remaining decisions—the choice of the color and kind of yarn, the stitches, the size of the rectangles—offer you ample opportunity to arrive at a unique solution that reflects your personal taste.

Lesson 1
How to Make the Modular Pullover

In Modular Crochet all pullovers are made from six or eight rectangles (six if they are sleeveless, eight if they have sleeves), and, for all styles, the procedure for putting them together is exactly the same. This lesson shows how the rectangles are joined together. All garments made following this method are worked in the ridge stitch. The main instructions are for the double crochet ridge stitch (dcr) and the half double crochet ridge stitch (hdcr); and the procedure is the same for both stitches. When working in the single crochet ridge stitch (scr), the number in the parentheses (x) tells you what to do. If you have any questions about abbreviations, stitches, detailing, consult the section *About Stitches and Detailing.* In our instructions you will note that there are no measurements or numbers of stitches given. This is because in Modular Crochet we have done away with gauge and measuring in the usual sense and teach you through photographs and diagrams how to work directly on your body. In this lesson the photographs will be your primary guide. To work from them, note in each step *where* and *how* the beginning chain and the rectangles of the garment fall on the body. Then work your beginning center chain and all subsequent rectangles so that they fall on the same places on your body. The text tells how many chains to turn and how to join the rectangles. That is all that you have to keep in mind, aside from being sure that the fabric is worked at the right tension. It is best to work each set of rectangles simultaneously (rectangles 1 through 4—center front and back, rectangles 5 and 6—sides, rectangles 7 and 8—sleeves). To do this, work rectangle 1 close to the width you think you want, then work rectangle 2 to the same width. Hold the piece up to your body. If you need more width, add a row at a time on each side until you get the desired width. Then work rectangles 3 and 4 to the same size. Crochet the other two sets (sides and sleeves) in the same way. Working in this way you can easily see how the fabric hangs and behaves, and you can get a good fit. This lesson is the key to the modular approach. Once you finish it, you will be able to make all of the styles shown in this book in all of the stitches by following the exact same procedures. You will also be prepared to work and design on your own.

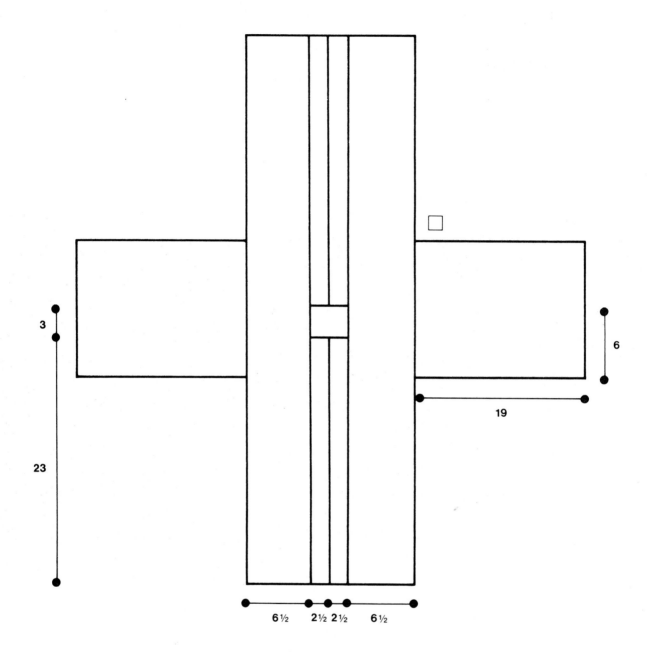

Materials: Paternayan Worsted or any good knitting worsted (4 oz skns): 6 in the color of your choice. Total Yardage: 1600. Hook: Size G or size to obtain gauge. Gauge: 4 dcr = 1″. Stitch: Dcr. Size: 5′6″, 34-24-34. The basic pullover is made with a square neck and medium width rectangles. We have used a plain knitting worsted, a medium weight yarn, because it is easy to work with; but you can use any yarn you like. Directions are for the half double crochet and double crochet ridge stitches. Changes for the single crochet ridge stitch are in parentheses. Because you are guided by step-by-step photographs in this lesson, the diagram is not necessary. But if you would like to refer to it as you work along and want to know how to read and use it, *Lesson 3* tells you how. The person making the pullover in our photographs is 5′6″, and her measurements are 34-24-34. As explained in *Lesson 3,* if you are the same size as the model, you can follow the diagram sizes as they are given. If not, the diagram shows how the rectangles have to be proportioned in order to get the effect shown in the photograph.

Rectangle 1

Starting at the center front,
work a chain to the desired length from the hem
to the bottom of the neck opening edge.

NOTE: The working of row 1, the next step, will alter the length of the chained piece; it will usually stretch as the stitches are worked in. To make allowances for this, work the chain a little longer (about 2 inches) than you think you will need. Then, after row 1 is worked in and the true length is reached, any extra chains can be removed by inserting a crochet hook into the last loop of the chain and pulling the loops out one by one. See page 178. To keep the true length of your piece as the rows are worked, read about maintaining tension in *About Stitches and Detailing*.

Row 1

Work one dc in the 3rd (2nd) chain
from the hook
and in each chain across.
Toward the end of the row,
hold the crocheted strip
up to your body
to see how you feel about the length.
Add a few stitches at a time
and check the length as you work along.
When it matches the length
in the photograph
or when it is the length that you want,
chain 2 (1), turn.

Next Rows

Working under only the back loop
(the loop further from you)
of each stitch
to make the ridge stitch,
work one stitch in the 3rd (2nd) loop from hook
and in each stitch across.
At the end of each row
chain 2 (1) to turn.
As the rows are worked,
hold the piece up to your body
to check on the width.
Use the photograph as a guide.
Consulting the diagram on page 10,
you will see that our rectangle
is 2½ inches wide in order to get the right fit.
When the desired width is reached,
cut the yarn and fasten it.

Rectangle 2

Row 1

Return to row 1 of rectangle 1.
At the end,
with the tail of the beginning chain protruding,
pull a loop through the loop
at the bottom of the first stitch.
Chain 3 (2).
Work one stitch in each loop across.
Do not work into the chain at the end of the row.
Chain 2 (1), turn.

NOTE: The loops you are working into are actually the loops left over from
the beginning chain when you worked row 1.

Row 2

Working under only the back loop
of each stitch,
make one stitch in each stitch across,
working the last stitch
in the top loop of the chain 3 (2)
at the end of the row.

Next Rows:

Work the same as rectangle 1.

Neck Opening

When the last stitch in rectangle 2 is complete
work a chain
to the top of the shoulder
until the desired neck opening depth is reached.
Consulting the diagram on page 10,
you will see that we have chained for 3 inches.
To end the chain, cut the yarn
and pull the end thread out.

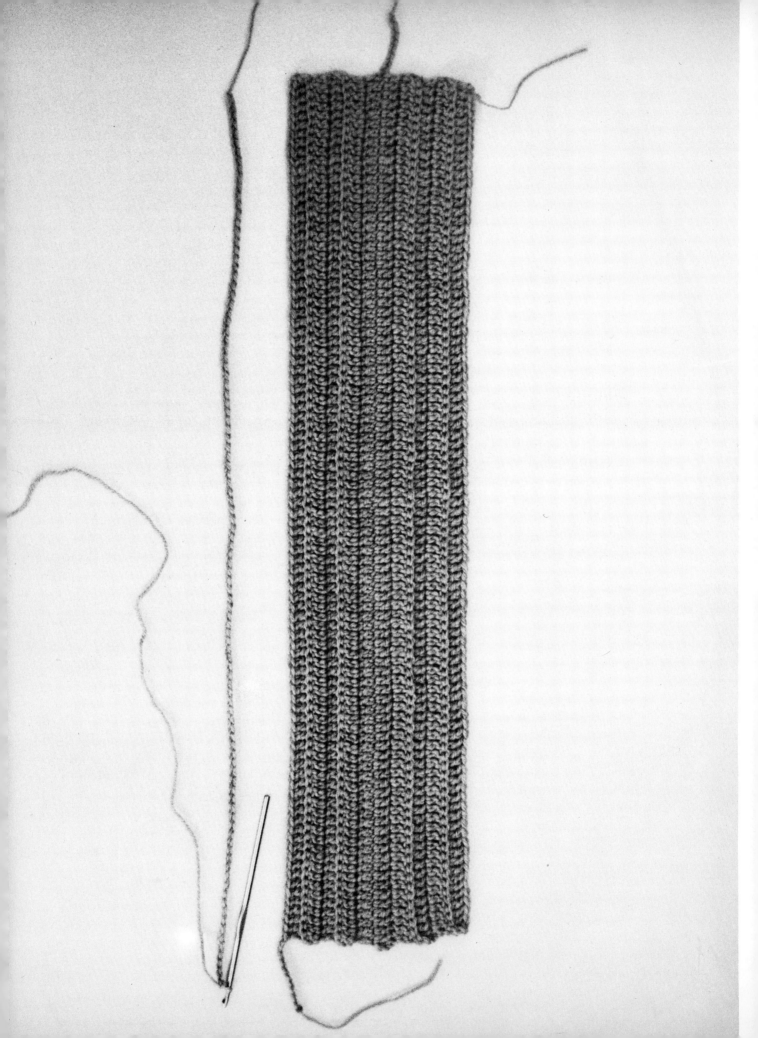

Rectangle 3

Back

Count the number of stitches
in the last row of rectangle 2
and the number of chains
for the neck opening.
Chain this total amount
for the center back chain.
For example,
our pullover has 94 stitches
in the last row of rectangle 2
plus 12 chains for the neck opening.
The sum of the two is 106.
Therefore, we chained 106
for the center back chain.

Next Rows

Work the same amount of rows
as in rectangle 2.
Then cut the yarn
and fasten it.

Rectangle 4

Row 1

Return to row 1 of rectangle 3.
At the end,
with the tail of the beginning chain protruding,
pull a loop through the loop
at the bottom of the first stitch.
Chain 3 (2).
Work the same as rectangle 3.
When the last row is complete,
chain the same amount of stitches
for the neck opening
as you did for rectangle 2.
To end the chain, cut the yarn
and pull the end thread out.

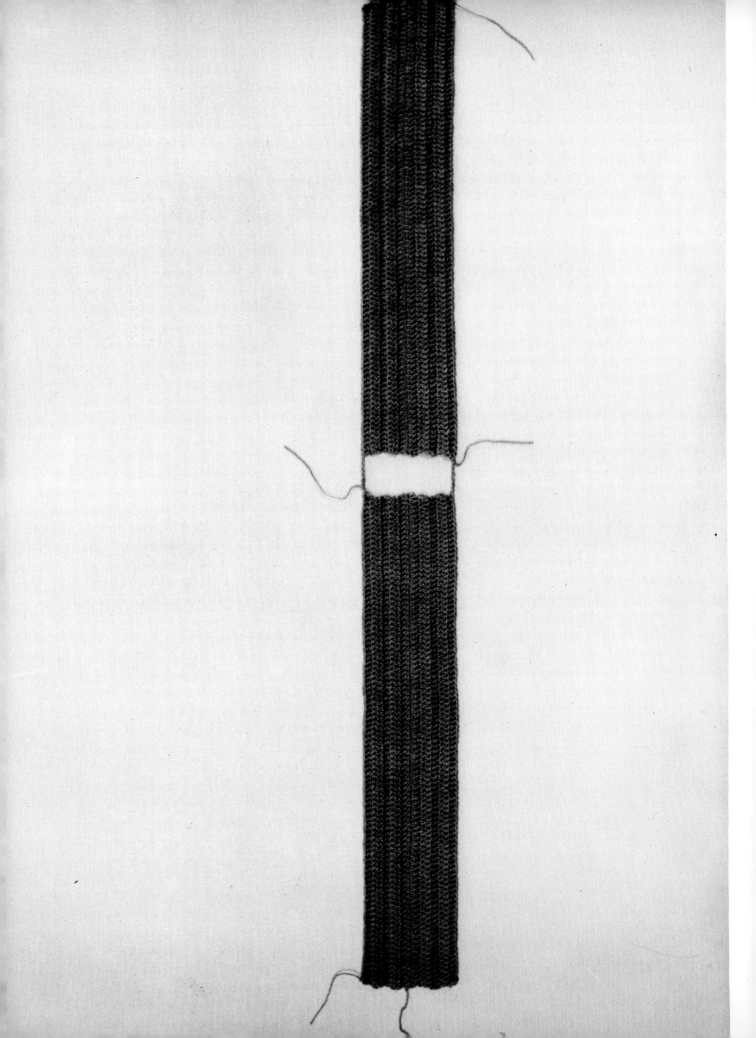

Join Front to Back

With a crochet hook,
and being careful not to twist the chain,
join the neck chain of rectangle 2
to the neck edge corner stitch
on the last row of rectangle 3.
Join the neck chain of rectangle 4
to the neck edge corner stitch
on the last row of rectangle 1.

NOTE: The section *About Stitches and Detailing* tells how to join the neck
chain to the crocheted piece with a loop. At this point the width of the rectangles can still be changed. If you feel the neck opening should be a little
wider or smaller, just take the chains for the neck opening out and add or
subtract the necessary amount of rows until you get the fit you want. Then
replace the chains and join the front to the back.

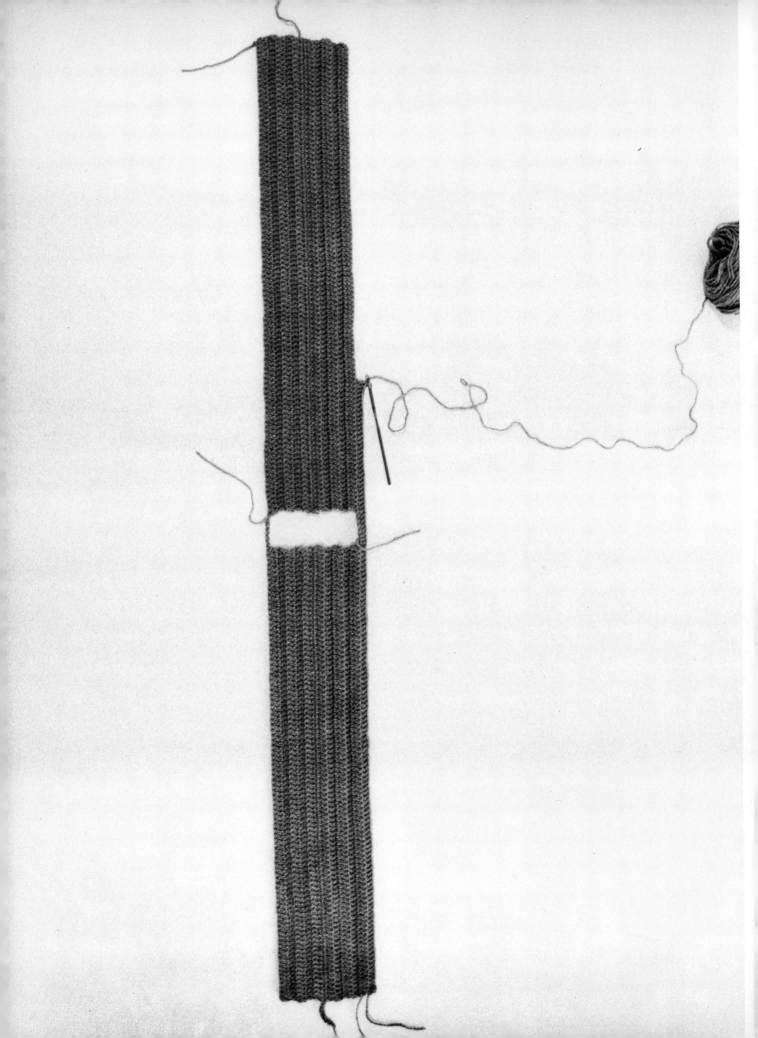

Rectangle 5

Row 1

Starting where you left off on rectangle 1—
with the wrong side of the stitch facing you—
pull a loop through the back loop
of the first stitch in the row.
Chain 3 (2). Do not count this chain as a stitch.
Work one stitch
into the same opening
as the chain.
Working under only the back loop
of each stitch,
work along the edge of rectangle 1,
work into the chains for the neck opening,
work along the edge of rectangle 4.
Chain 2 (1), turn.

NOTE: The section *About Stitches and Detailing* tells how to read the right
and wrong side of the stitches.

Next Rows

Work in the ridge stitch.
Try the garment on
as you work along
to see how it fits.
Compare it with the photograph.
When the desired width is reached,
cut the yarn and fasten it.
Consulting the diagram on page 10,
you will see
that in order to get the right fit,
we made our rectangle 6½ inches wide.

Rectangle 6

Row 1

Starting where you left off on rectangle 3—
with the wrong side of the stitch facing you—
pull a loop through the back loop
of the first stitch in the row.
Chain 3 (2). Do not count this chain as a stitch.
Work one stitch
into the same opening
as the chain,
then work in the same way as rectangle 5.
Cut the yarn and fasten it.

NOTE: At this point you can still make adjustments. To check the fit, baste
the seams loosely and try the garment on. If you want to change the width,
add or subtract the necessary amount of rows until you get the fit you want.

Fold the garment in half at the shoulders.
On right side of fabric,
starting at the bottom edge
whipstitch the side seams
(See *About Stitches and Detailing*)
until the armhole opening
is the size
that you want the sleeve to be.
Consulting the diagram you will see that our sleeve
and therefore our sleeve opening
is 6 inches wide.

NOTE: Either side of the garment can be made the right side. If the right side
of row 1 is used as the right side, you will get a slight indentation at the center
of the garment. If the wrong side of row 1 is used as the right side, you will get
a raised ridge. Compare the two sides of your garment to see what we mean.
We have made the right side the side with the indentation.

Rectangle 7

Sleeve in the Round—Round 1:
Starting at the armhole bottom,
with the wrong side of the stitch facing you,
pull a loop through the back loop
of the first stitch.
Chain 3 (2).

NOTE: The sleeves (rectangles 7 and 8) can be worked in two ways, flat or in the round. If you do not know how to work in the round as we have done, do make an effort to learn how. In the long run, working in the round with all types of yarns is easier and quicker. And, more importantly, the seam formed is far superior to one that is sewn or woven; it looks good both inside and out. This is especially desirable when the garment has a fold-up cuff. The section *About Stitches and Detailing* has comprehensive drawings (pages 182-3) that show how to work in the round. However, some beginners at first prefer to work flat, especially when working with textured yarns where the stitches are harder to read. If you would rather work flat, see the next "note" section for the steps to follow.

Round 1 (continued)

Working in the ridge stitch,
work one stitch in each stitch around.
When the last stitch of the round is complete,
insert the hook
into the top of the beginning chain 3 (2).
Then join with a slip stitch
by placing the yarn over and drawing the yarn
through the chain *and* the loop on the hook.

NOTE: To work the sleeve flat do not join with a slip stitch. Instead, at the end
of row 1, chain 2 (1) and then work the next rows in the usual manner for flat
pieces. When the sleeve is complete, fold it in half and slip stitch or sew the
seam.

Round 2

Chain 2 (1).
Turn the work to the other side
so that the wrong side of the stitch is facing you.
Work the first stitch under only the back loop
of the first stitch in the round—
the 4th (3rd) loop from hook.
Work one stitch in each stitch around,
making the last stitch
in the top of the last stitch
of the previous round.
Do not work into the chain or you will add a stitch.
Join with a slip stitch
into the top of the beginning chain.

Next Rounds

Repeat the steps in round 2
until the desired sleeve length is reached.

Sleeve Trim

For the hdcr and dcr work one row of the scr
on right side of fabric.
Then cut the yarn and join with a loop.
The section *About Stitches and Detailing* tells you how.

Rectangle 8

Second Sleeve

Work the same as the first sleeve.
Before starting, count the stitches to make sure
there are the same number as on the first sleeve.
If there is a difference, add or remove
some of the whip stitches in the seam.
Since you are working from the shoulder down,
it is easy to adjust the length of the sleeve.
If it stretches, take some rows out.
If it needs to be longer
or you decide you want a cuff, add some rows.

Neck Trim

On right side of fabric
work 1 scr in each stitch along side edges,
work 2 (1) scr around the end stitch of each row
along the front and back edges.

Lesson 2
How to Make the Different Neck Styles

All the classic neck treatments are possible with the modular method. *Lesson 1* showed you how to make the basic pullover which has a square neck. The following step-by-step diagrams show you how to make four variations of this basic neckline: round, boat, V necks, and turtlenecks or hoods. These neck style variations are achieved by altering rectangles 1 through 4 in some way. To follow the step-by-step diagrams, make the beginning center front chain to suit the style and to fit your body or the body of the person for whom you are making the garment. Then join the rectangles as shown in each drawing. If you need more specific information on a particular aspect of a step—how many chains to turn, how the rectangles are joined, or other details—refer back to the photographs in *Lesson 1*. For the round neck, you increase at the neck edge every few rows. Usually you have to increase three or four times for the front (rectangles 1 and 2) and only once, on the last row, for the back (rectangles 3 and 4). Then you add the rest of the rectangles (5 through 8) in the usual way. The boat neck is the easiest variation to make. Make the beginning center chain the length of the garment from hem to neck edge and the same size for both the front (rectangles 1 and 2) and the back (rectangles 3 and 4). When they are complete you join them at the neck. Add rectangles 5 and 6 by crocheting into all of the stitches along the edges of rectangles 1 and 4, then 2 and 3. Add rectangles 7 and 8 if sleeves are desired. Make the V neck by working rectangles 1 through 4 only one row wide (except for halter-type garments for reasons explained in *Lesson 4*). The neck chain is worked 2 inches longer than usual to make a deeper opening in the back so the garment will hang properly. Add rectangles 5 and 6 and rectangles 7 and 8 in the usual way. Make turtlenecks and hoods by working rectangles 1 through 4 extra long and working each set (1 and 2, 3 and 4) to the same size. Then sew the upper parts together down to the shoulder to make a tube. Crochet rectangle 5 into the unworked stitches of rectangles 1 and 4. Crochet rectangle 6 into the unworked stitches of rectangles 2 and 3. Whipstitch the side seams and add rectangles 7 and 8 if desired. The following step-by-step diagrams explain in detail what to do.

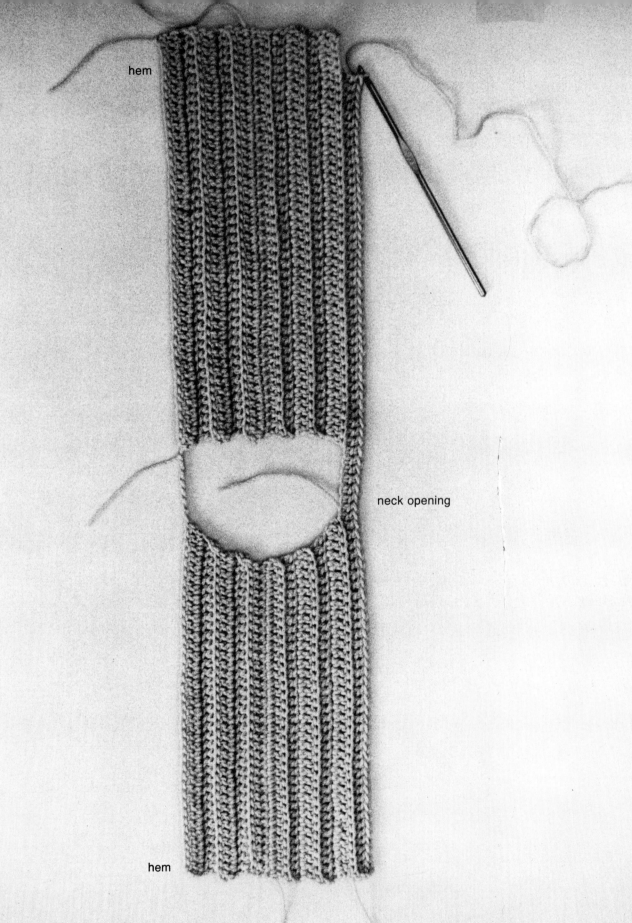

hem

neck opening

hem

Rectangles 1 through 4 are shown completed with the front and back joined; steps 1 through 9.
Row 1 of rectangle 5 is shown partly worked in; step 10.

How to Make a Round Neck

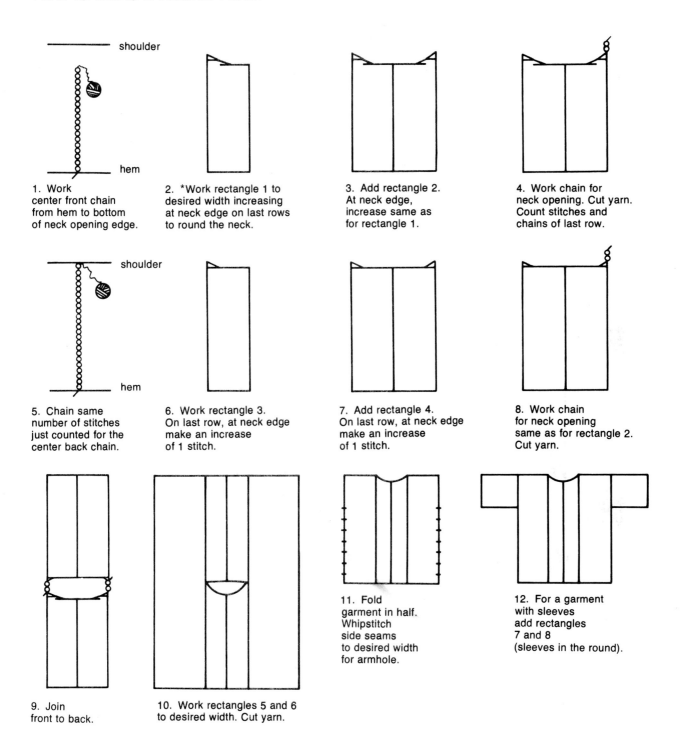

1. Work center front chain from hem to bottom of neck opening edge.

2. *Work rectangle 1 to desired width increasing at neck edge on last rows to round the neck.

3. Add rectangle 2. At neck edge, increase same as for rectangle 1.

4. Work chain for neck opening. Cut yarn. Count stitches and chains of last row.

5. Chain same number of stitches just counted for the center back chain.

6. Work rectangle 3. On last row, at neck edge make an increase of 1 stitch.

7. Add rectangle 4. On last row, at neck edge make an increase of 1 stitch.

8. Work chain for neck opening same as for rectangle 2. Cut yarn.

9. Join front to back.

10. Work rectangles 5 and 6 to desired width. Cut yarn.

11. Fold garment in half. Whipstitch side seams to desired width for armhole.

12. For a garment with sleeves add rectangles 7 and 8 (sleeves in the round).

*To Round the Neck: Work the rows straight for a ½ inch or to where you want the curve to start. Then start to increase at the neck edge by working 2 stitches in the same opening in the last stitch of the row. To get the smoothest curve, it is best to increase on every other row or to increase on every other row and then on every row for the last rows (the sample on the left is increased on rows 2, 4 and 5). If you are in doubt about how often to increase, make a little swatch about ½ inch high and work it to the width of rectangle 1, trying different increases at the neck edge until you get the desired curve. This takes only a few minutes and may save you a lot of time.

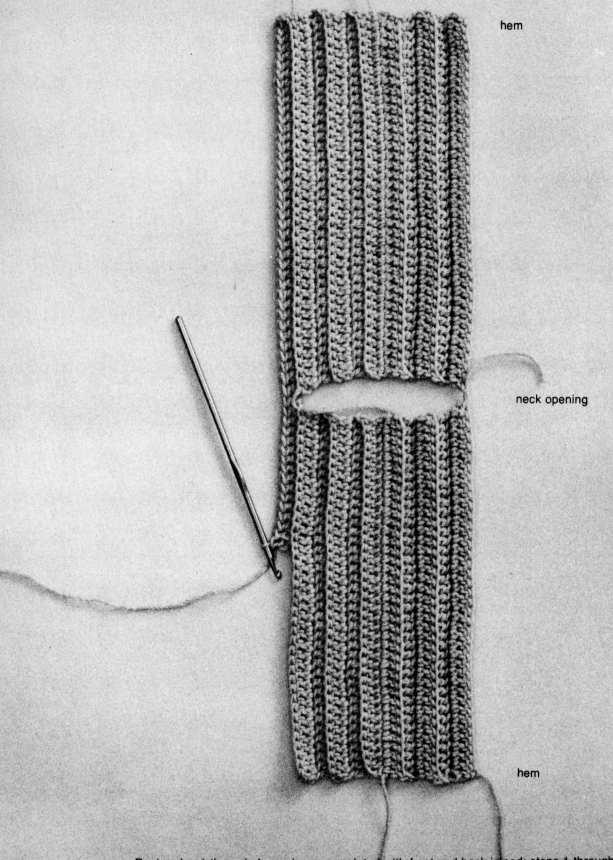

hem

neck opening

hem

Rectangles 1 through 4 are shown completed with front and back joined; steps 1 through 5.
Row 1 of rectangle 5 is shown partly worked in; step 6.

How to Make a Boat Neck

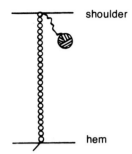

1. Work center front chain from hem to bottom of neck opening edge.

2. Work rectangle 1 to desired width. Cut yarn.

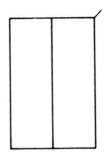

3. Return to center front. Starting at end with tail of beginning chain protruding, work rectangle 2. Cut yarn.

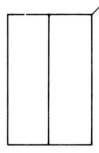

4. Work rectangles 3 and 4 same as rectangles 1 and 2.

5. Join front to back. Try the garment on to see if the width is correct. Make adjustments if necessary.

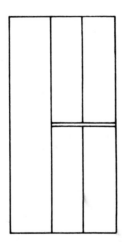

6. Rectangle 5—Row 1: Work along edge of rectangle 1, then work along edge of rectangle 4. Work to desired width. Cut yarn.

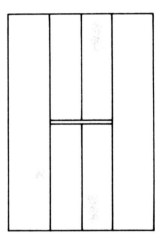

7. Work rectangle 6 same as rectangle 5. Cut yarn.

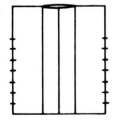

8. Fold garment in half. Whipstitch side seams to desired width for armhole.

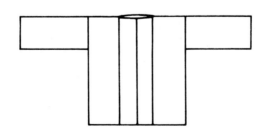

9. For a garment with sleeves work rectangles 7 and 8 (sleeves in the round).

53

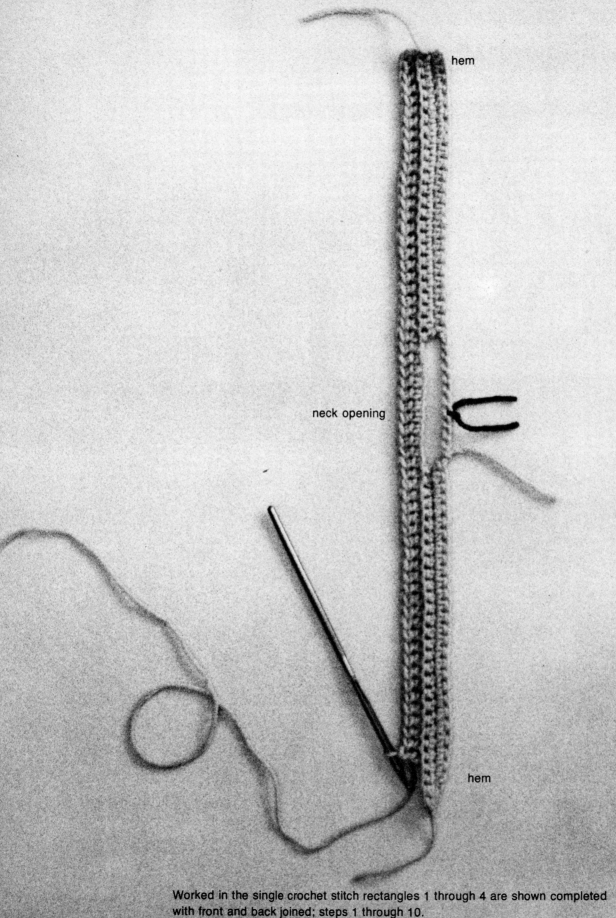

hem

neck opening

hem

Worked in the single crochet stitch rectangles 1 through 4 are shown completed with front and back joined; steps 1 through 10.
Row 1 of rectangle 5 is shown partly worked in; step 11.

How to Make a V Neck

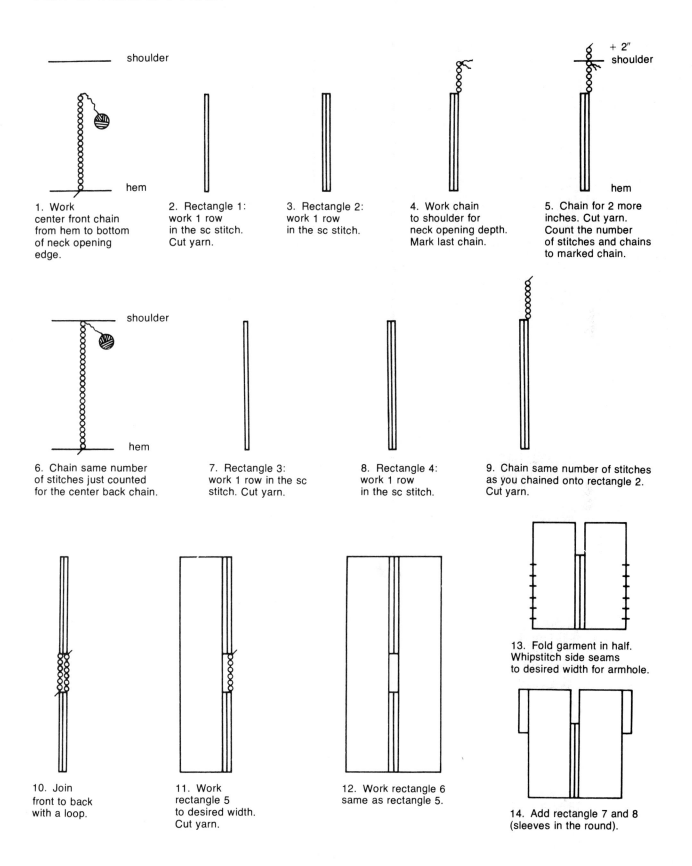

shoulder

hem

1. Work center front chain from hem to bottom of neck opening edge.

2. Rectangle 1: work 1 row in the sc stitch. Cut yarn.

3. Rectangle 2: work 1 row in the sc stitch.

4. Work chain to shoulder for neck opening depth. Mark last chain.

+ 2"
shoulder

hem

5. Chain for 2 more inches. Cut yarn. Count the number of stitches and chains to marked chain.

shoulder

hem

6. Chain same number of stitches just counted for the center back chain.

7. Rectangle 3: work 1 row in the sc stitch. Cut yarn.

8. Rectangle 4: work 1 row in the sc stitch.

9. Chain same number of stitches as you chained onto rectangle 2. Cut yarn.

10. Join front to back with a loop.

11. Work rectangle 5 to desired width. Cut yarn.

12. Work rectangle 6 same as rectangle 5.

13. Fold garment in half. Whipstitch side seams to desired width for armhole.

14. Add rectangle 7 and 8 (sleeves in the round).

Step 1:
Chain for a turtleneck.

Step 1:
Chain for a hood.

Step 5:
The front is shown
joined to the back
with the neck seams
whipstitched
to desired length.

Step 6:
Row 1
of rectangle 5
is shown partly
worked in.

How to Make a Turtleneck or Hood

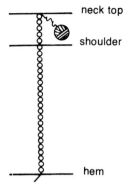

1. Work center front chain from hem to shoulder, then continue to chain for length of turtleneck or hood.*

2. Work rectangle 1 to desired width. Cut yarn.

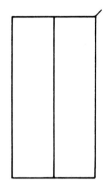

3. Work rectangle 2 to same width as rectangle 1. Cut yarn.

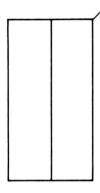

4. Work rectangles 3 and 4 same as rectangles 1 and 2.

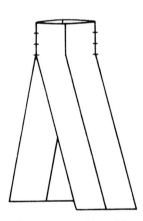

5. Place wrong sides of front and back together. Whipstitch side seams from top of neck to shoulder. Try the piece on to check width and length. If necessary, add or subtract rows or whipstitches until you get the width and length you want.

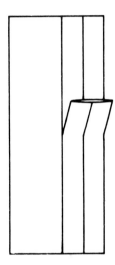

6. Rectangle 5—Row 1: Starting where you left off, work along edge of rectangle 1 to seam of turtleneck or hood, then work along edge of rectangle 4. Work to desired width. Cut yarn.

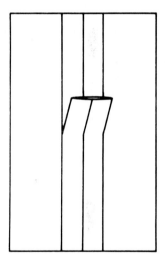

7. Work rectangle 6 same as rectangle 5. Try the piece on. Adjust the width if necessary. Cut yarn.

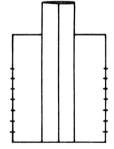

8. Fold garment in half. Whipstitch side seams to desired width for armhole.

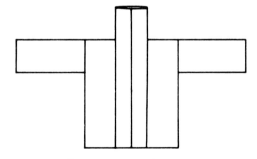

9. For a garment with sleeves work rectangles 7 and 8 (sleeves in the round).

*Consult the measurements in the diagrams of Lesson 4 to get an idea of how long the chain should be for different neck styles.

Lesson 3
How to Read and Use the Diagrams

There are seven different types of diagrams: square neck, round neck, V neck, boat neck, turtleneck or hood for the different neck variations; and the smocked silhouette and bloused silhouette for the shape variations. For easy referral when you are working in *Lesson 4* each type of diagram has an identifying symbol that you can match, on the upper right-hand corner; a square for the square neck, a circle for the round neck, and so on. Each diagram shows the garment as it would look if it were spread out flat. A diagram will have six rectangles if the garment is sleeveless, eight rectangles if the garment has sleeves. If working from a diagram is new to you, the call letters (a, b, c, etc.) explain what the measurements are for on the diagrams used in *Lesson 4.* In this method the diagrams take the place of the usual written instructions and should be used in conjunction with the photographs. Since all garments are made from the same six or eight rectangles what becomes important is the size and proportions of the rectangles, and this is the information that the diagram gives you. If you are the same size as the person in the photograph you can probably use the measurements and proportions as given. If not, you will have to alter the rectangles to fit your particular size. If you are an adult woman and the model is also an adult woman any changes made will probably occur in the lengths of the rectangles, rather than in the widths, since the main difference in the sizing of a garment is usually based on a person's height. However, if there is a considerable difference between your size and that of the model's, or if the garment in the photograph is on a child and you are making it for a man the differences in the size of the rectangles will be significant. In such cases the primary value of the diagram is to give you some idea of how the rectangles should be proportioned to one another in order to get the particular silhouette or effect shown in the size that you want. When designing garments on your own, use the diagrams for reference. The measurements and the proportions of the rectangles will give you an idea of what size the rectangles should be in order to get certain effects. For instance, they tell you how wide the sleeves usually are when the body is a certain width. If you want to know how a garment looks when it is 12, 20, or 30 inches wide or 14, 20, or 28 inches long, or what happens when a turtleneck is 8, 10, or 12 inches wide, find the photograph that comes closest to the style you have in mind and examine the measurements and proportions of the rectangles in the diagram. If you want to know what would happen if the rectangles were longer or narrower than what you have in mind consult the diagrams and the photographs and compare them.

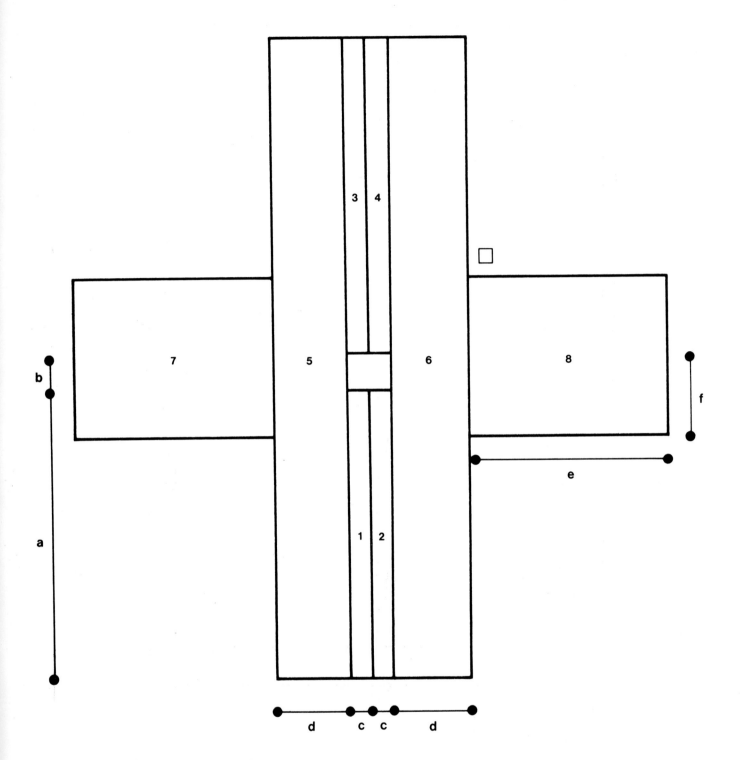

Diagram for Square Necks

a is the length of rectangle 1 from hem to bottom edge of neck opening.
b is the depth of the neck opening.
c is the width of rectangles 1 through 4.
d is the width of rectangles 5 and 6.
e is the width of the armholes and sleeves when the garment is folded in half.
f is the length of the sleeves—rectangles 7 and 8.

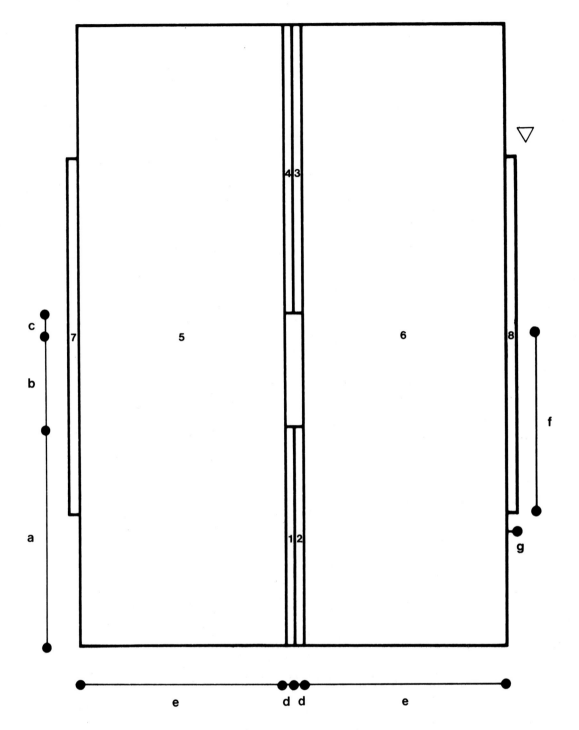

Diagram for V Necks

a is the length of rectangle 1 from hem to bottom edge of neck opening.
b is the depth of the front neck opening.
c is the additional amount to chain for the back neck opening.
d is the width of rectangles 1 through 4.
e is the width of rectangles 5 and 6.
f is the width of the armholes and sleeves when the garment is folded in half.
g is the length of the sleeves—rectangles 7 and 8.

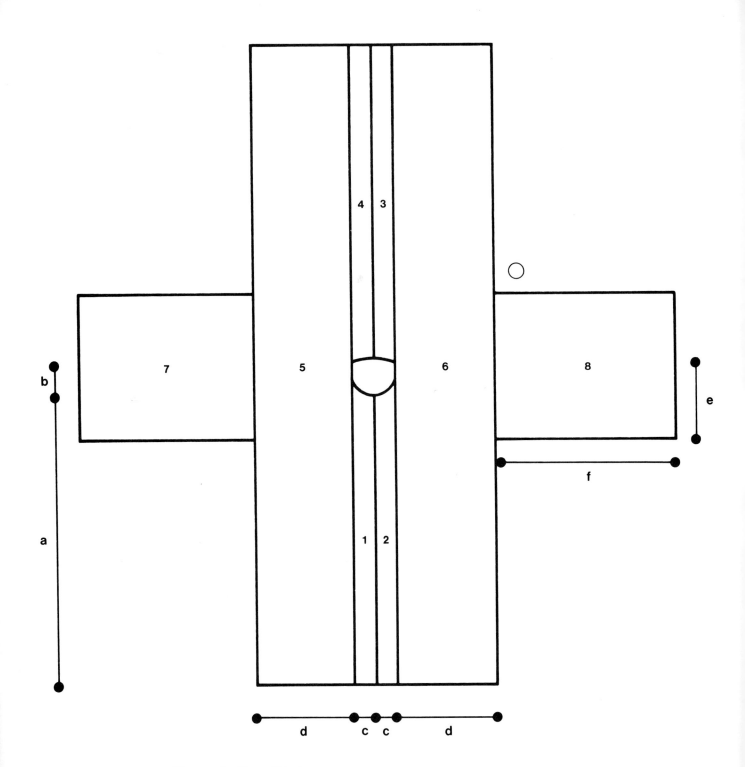

Diagram for Round Necks

a is the length of rectangle 1 before the increases start.
b is the depth of the neck opening from the lowest point to the shoulder.
c is the width of rectangles 1 through 4.
d is the width of rectangles 5 and 6.
e is the width of the armholes and sleeves when the garment is folded in half.
f is the length of the sleeves—rectangles 7 and 8.

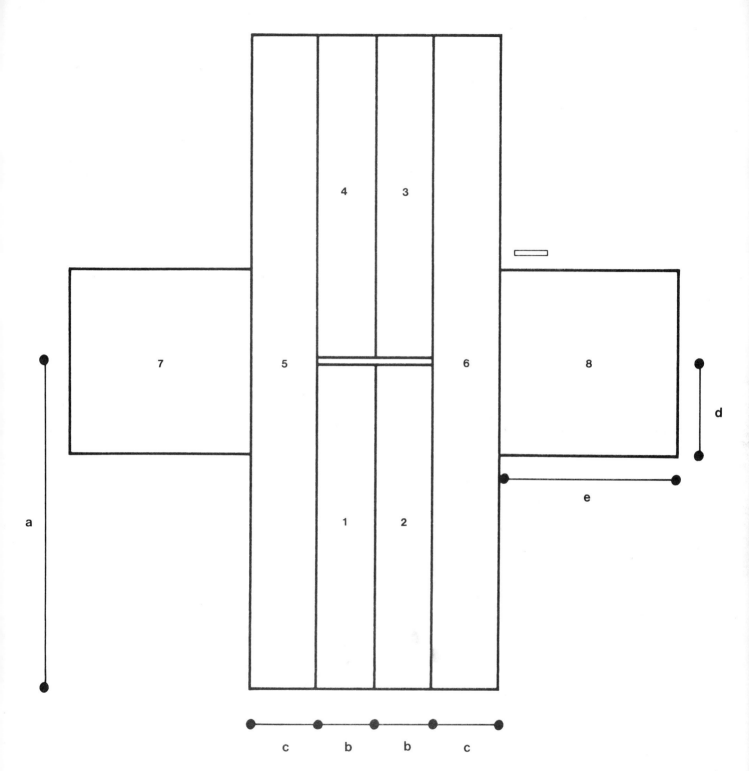

Diagram for Boat Necks

a is the length of rectangles 1 through 4 from hem to neck opening edge.
b is the width of rectangles 1 through 4.
c is the width of rectangles 5 and 6.
d is the width of the armholes and sleeves when the garment is folded in half.
e is the length of the sleeves—rectangles 7 and 8.

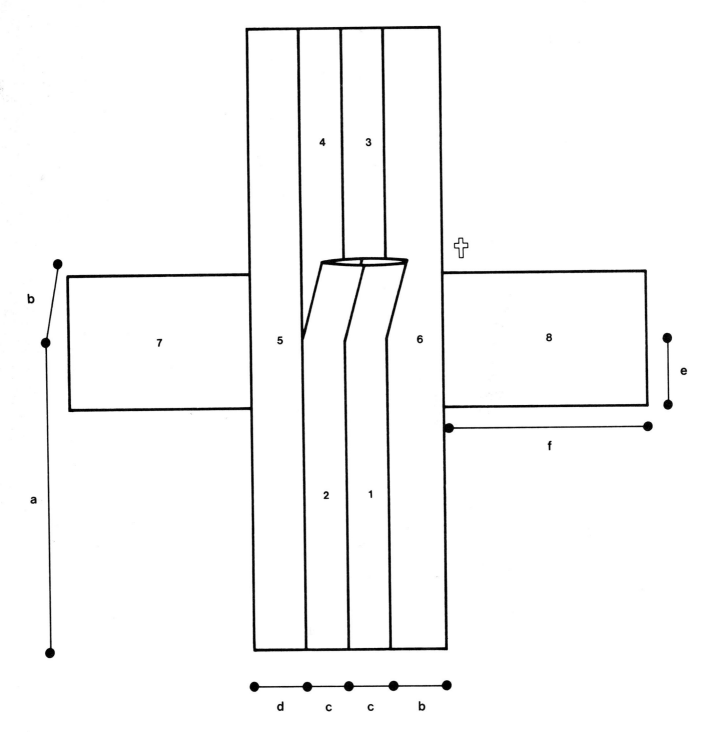

Diagram for Turtlenecks or Hoods

a is the length of rectangles 1 through 4 from hem to shoulder.
b is the length of the turtleneck or hood from shoulder to top edge.
a plus b is the total length of rectangles 1 through 4.
c is the width of rectangles 1 through 4.
d is the width of rectangles 5 and 6.
e is the width of the armholes and sleeves when the garment is folded in half.
f is the length of the sleeves—rectangles 7 and 8.

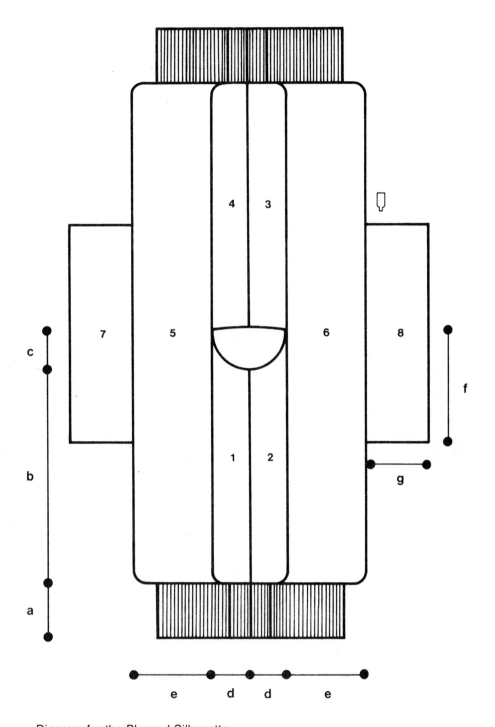

Diagram for the Bloused Silhouette

a plus b is the total length of rectangles 1 and 2.
a, the shaded section, is the number of inches to work in the shorter stitch.
b, the unshaded section, is the number of inches to work in the longer stitch.
c is the depth of the neck opening.
d is the width of rectangles 1 through 4 at their widest part.
e is the width of rectangles 5 and 6 at their widest part.
f is the width of the armholes and sleeves when the garment is folded in half.
g is the length of the sleeves—rectangles 7 and 8.

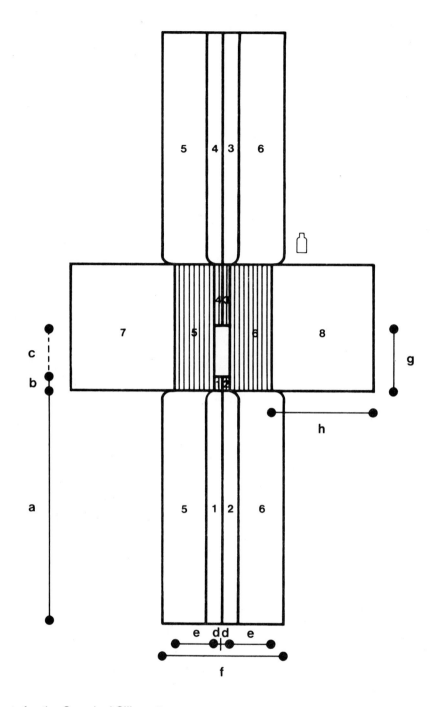

Diagram for the Smocked Silhouette

a plus b is the total length of rectangles 1 and 2.
a, the unshaded section, is the number of inches to work in the longer stitch to make the skirt.
b, the shaded section, is the number of inches to work in the shorter stitch to make the bodice.
c is the depth of the neck opening.
d is the width of rectangles 1 through 4 at their narrowest part.
e is the width of rectangles 5 and 6 at their narrowest part.
f is the total width of the skirt.
g is the width of the armholes and sleeves when the garment is folded in half.
h is the length of the sleeves—rectangles 7 and 8.

Lesson 4
How to Work from Photographs and Diagrams

Lesson 4 is designed to be used as a workbook. Each project can be handled in one of two ways: you can either recreate the style exactly as it is shown, or you can use the themes and silhouettes as points of departure for making up designs of your own. Here is how you proceed in order to recreate, in your own size, or in someone else's the styles shown. The text under the diagram gives all the information needed to make the garment up in that particular size. If the hook size given does not give the gauge or effect that you want use the hook size that works for your hand. You do not have to use the yarn recommended but can substitute any yarn as long as it suits the silhouette and styling. If you substitute a yarn of the same thickness you can use the yardage amount that is given. If you use a yarn of a different thickness, or if you are making the garment up in a different size the yardage needed will most likely be different. *About Yarn* describes several ways to get the yard-age figures you will need. As they were in *Lesson 1* the photographs will again be your primary guide. To start work, note in the photograph how and especially where the rectangles of the garment fall on the body. Then work your beginning center chain and all subsequent rectangles so that they will fall on the same places on your body (unless you are changing the propor-tions for some reason). Again, it is best to work the corresponding rectangles simultaneously (1 through 4, 5 and 6, 7 and 8), so you can try on the garment as you work along and can see how it looks and fits. As the rows are added, compare the garment to the photograph and to the proportions of the rect-angles in the diagram. The measurements given there will give you an idea of how the rectangles should be sized in order to get the same effect and styling as shown. If you forget a step refer back to *Lesson 1* and *Lesson 2.* To find the right type of diagram if you refer back to *Lesson 3* match the symbol that is on the upper right-hand corner of each diagram. To suggest variations for when you are working on your own, we have based each garment on a different theme. Some of the themes shown are variations in silhouette (different neck styles, different body and sleeve widths, smocked and bloused silhouettes). Other themes show various fabric treatments (mixed yarns, stitch, and stripe patterns). In addition, each garment is crocheted in a yarn of a different thickness and type which should prove particularly helpful to crocheters who are not aware of the extraordinary range of yarns available for crocheting or how the yarns look and behave as fabrics once they are made up.

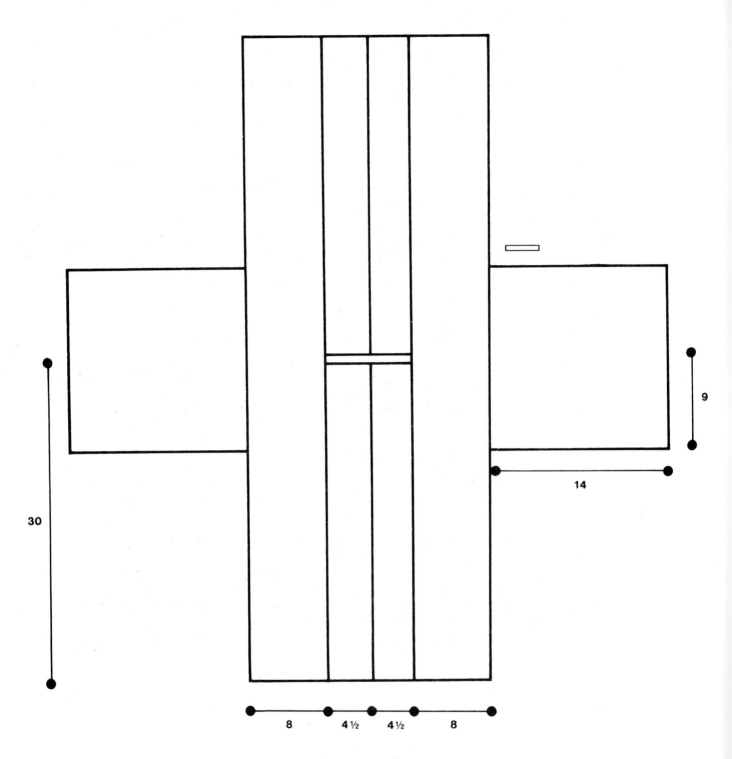

Make each set of rectangles in a different stitch.

Materials: Natural Irish Wool (2 oz skns): 12 natural. Total Yardage: 1500. Hook: Size J. Gauge: 6 hdcr = 2″. Stitches: Scr, hdcr, dcr. Size: 5′6″, 34-24-34. Rectangles 1 through 4: Work in the hdcr. Rectangles 5 and 6: Work in the scr. Rectangles 7 and 8 (sleeves): Work in the dcr. When mixing different stitches you may find that the sizes of the rectangles will vary slightly. To correct this, block the garment as described in the section *About Yarn. See* page 68, left.

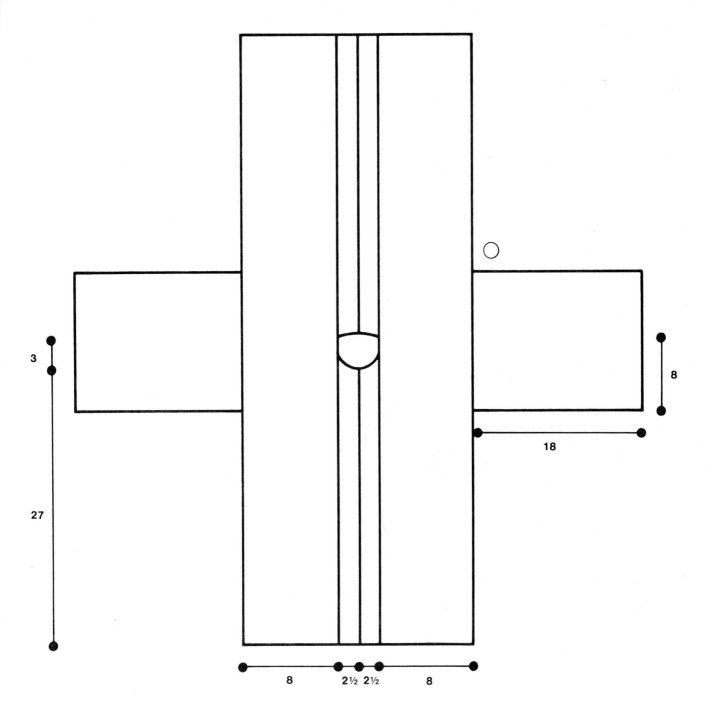

Pullovers made from rectangles
make free and easy shapes with loose, flowing lines.

Materials: Icelandic Homespun (50 gram skns): 15 dark brown. Total Yardage: 1785. Hook: Size H. Gauge: 7 scr = 2″. Stitch: Scr. Size: 5′6″, 34-24-34. A pullover 14 inches wide makes a clinging garment that shows the body's natural curves. Worked to 16 inches, the fabric rests lightly on the surface of the body in such a way that the curves beneath are still visible. At 18 inches the fabric starts to hang loose. At 20 inches it hangs free, and the lines of the fabric are straight. At 24 inches or over, the fabric begins to drape into folds making a dramatic silhouette with clean, fluid lines. *See* page 68, right.

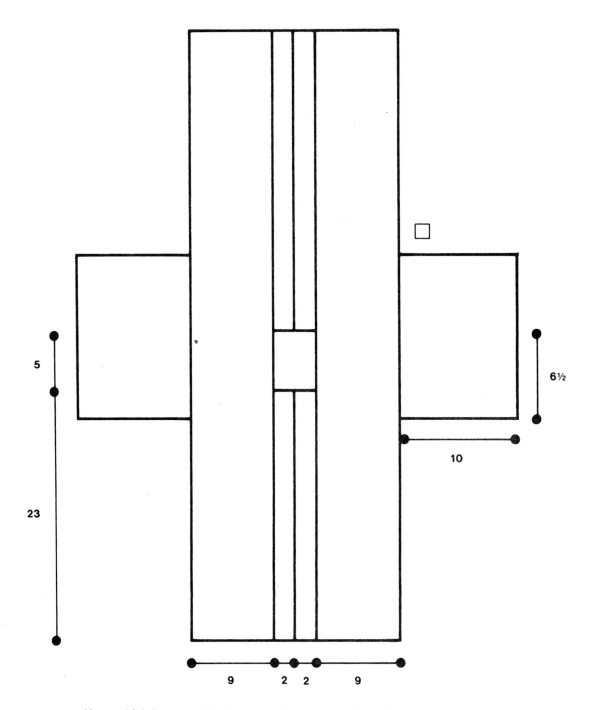

5

6½

23

10

9   2   2   9

Unusual fabrics are a simple way to alter the modular pullover, but if you cannot find a yarn that pleases you, make up one of your own for a one-of-a-kind fabric.

Materials: Gleneagle Fingering Yarn (1 oz skns): 12 each of black and camel. Total Yardage: 2520 yards of each color. Hook: Size J. Gauge: 3 scr = 1". Stitch: Scr. Size: 5'6", 34-24-34. Mixing yarns makes it possible for crocheters to custom design their own yarn just as the spinners do. The yarns can be put together in numerous ways, combining 2, 5, or 10 strands. You can make the yarns all the same or have each one be different. The subtle tweed for this sweater was achieved by combining four strands of the same type of yarn—two strands of each color—in two, low key colors. *See* page 69, left.

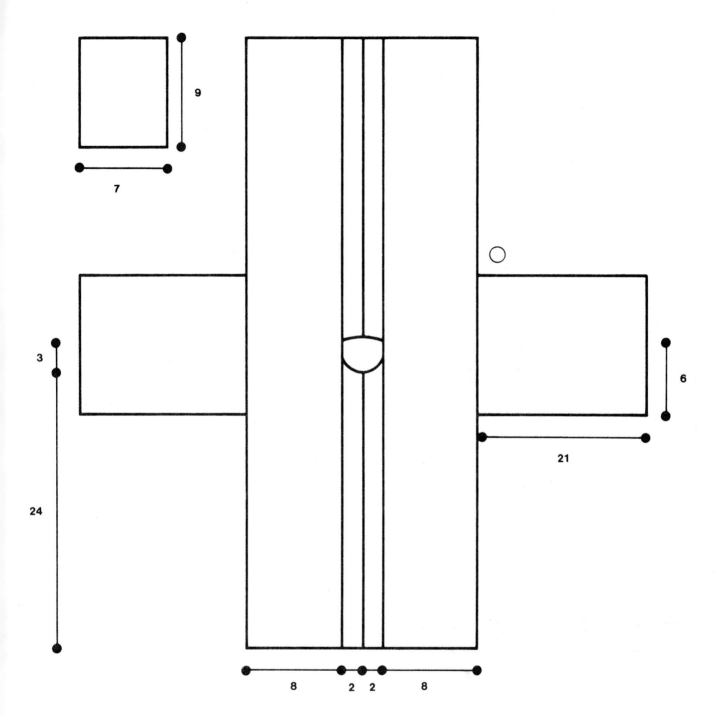

In this combination of yarns
each strand is a different thickness, color, and texture.

Materials: No. 1 Mohair (40 gram skns): 5 ivory. Gleneagle (1 oz skns): 5 caramel. Light weight Donegal (4 oz skns): 2 camel. Alpacka (3.5 oz skns): 1 medium brown. Total Yardage: 900 yards of each color. Hook: Size J. Gauge: 2 scr = 1″. Stitch: Scr. Size: 5′7″, 34-24-34. Note how the mohair in this mixing creates a cloudlike film over the surface of the fabric. If you are working with mixed yarns for the first time, take some scraps and make up a few swatches to acquaint yourself with the technique; also consult the section *About Yarn* for more information. *See* page 69, right.

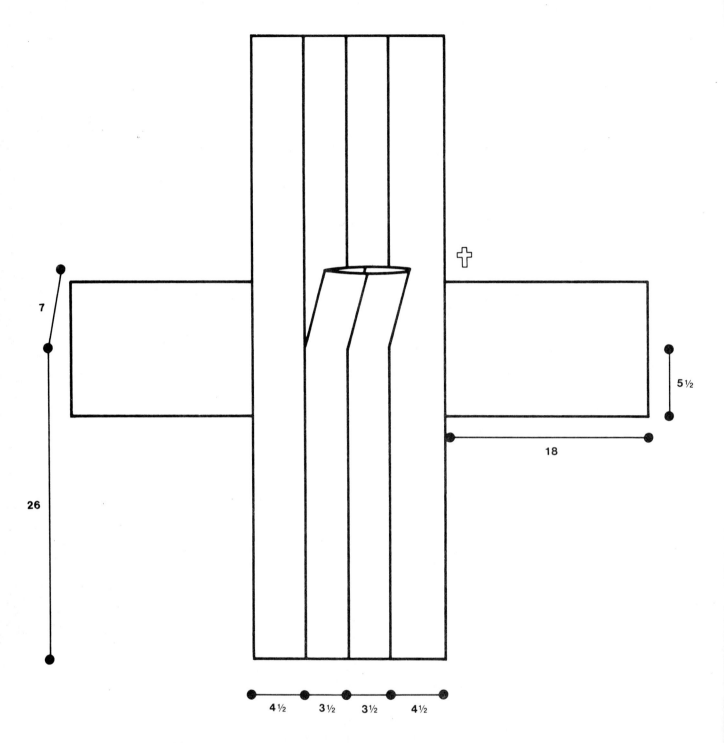

7

5½

26

18

4½   3½   3½   4½

Modular Crochet also makes possible a turtleneck of classic proportions.

Materials: Versaille Shetland Wool—(50 gram skns): 10 camel. Total Yardage: 1450. Hook: Size F. Gauge: 9 hdcr = 2″. Stitch: Hdcr. Size: 5′6″, 34-24-34. People who think that all crocheted fabrics are fancy and elaborate often assume that this sweater is knit. The plain ribbing of the half double crochet ridge stitch, worked in a classic yarn and color, makes a handsome and informal fabric with universal appeal. *Lesson 2* has step-by-step diagrams that show how rectangles 1 through 4 are altered in order to make the turtleneck shape.

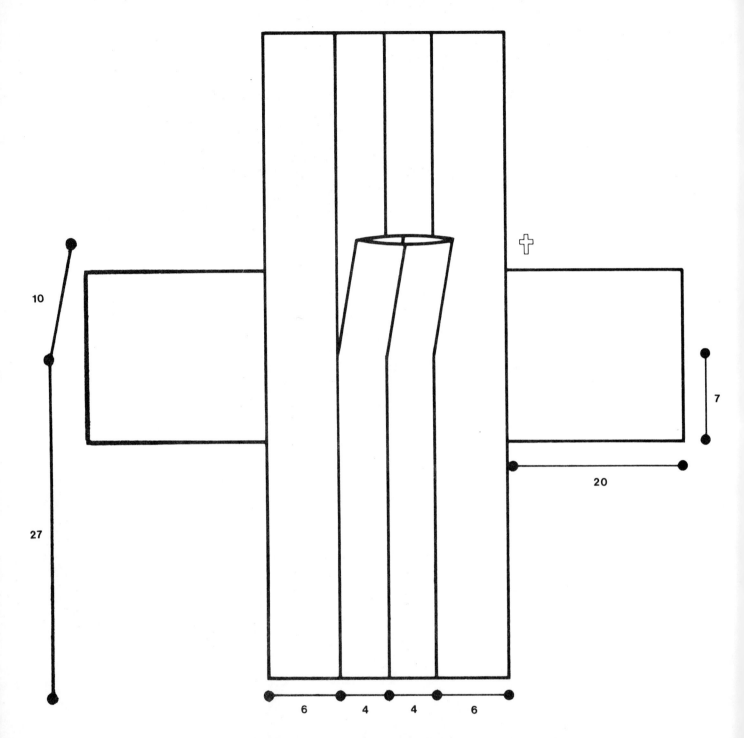

A nubby bouclé crocheted into a tube of medium width and length
makes a soft and graceful cowl neck.

Materials: Catkin (50 gram skns): 18 brown. Total Yardage: 1044. Hook: Size J.
Gauge: 5 scr = 2″. Stitch: Scr. Size: 5′7″, 34-24-34. If you are unsure about the
width of the neck when making a turtleneck or cowl neck, make the front (rectangles 1 and 2) and the back (rectangles 3 and 4) simultaneously. When you get
close to the width that you think you want, pin or baste the front and the back
together at the neck as each row is added and try the tube on to see how it looks.

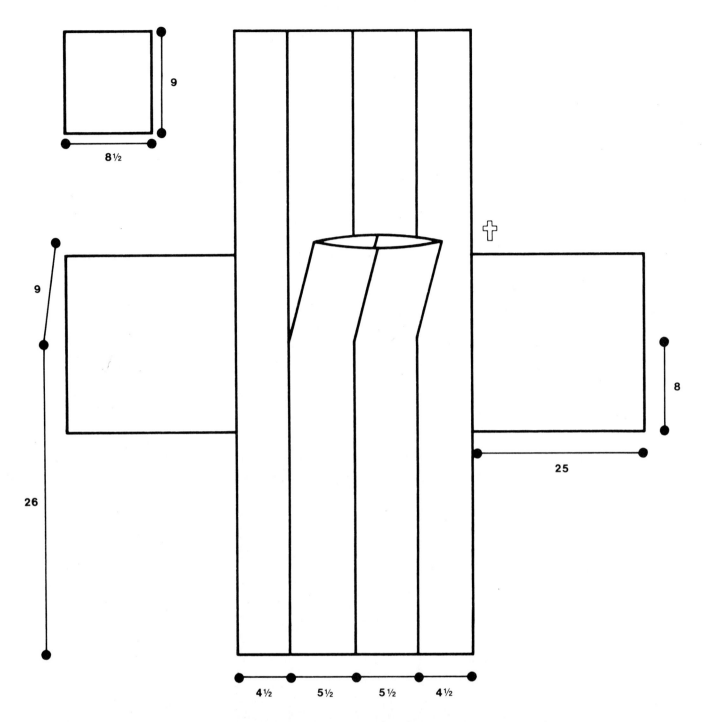

9

8½

9

8

25

26

4½   5½   5½   4½

All that is needed to make the modular pullover
exotic and different is a beautiful and unusual yarn.

Materials: Handspun Colombian Wool (8 oz skns): 8 mixed naturals. Total Yardage: 3520. Hook: Size J. Gauge: 5 scr = 2″. Stitch: Scr. Size: 5′6″, 34-24-34. The wool in this yarn is literally right off the sheep, with all the natural oils left in to make it waterproof. You may even find a few twigs, pebbles, or butterfly wings tucked among the strands. Because the wool is handspun and thick and thin, some find it difficult to crochet, but somehow the stitches all nestle into place, and it is not hard to work if you can read your stitches.

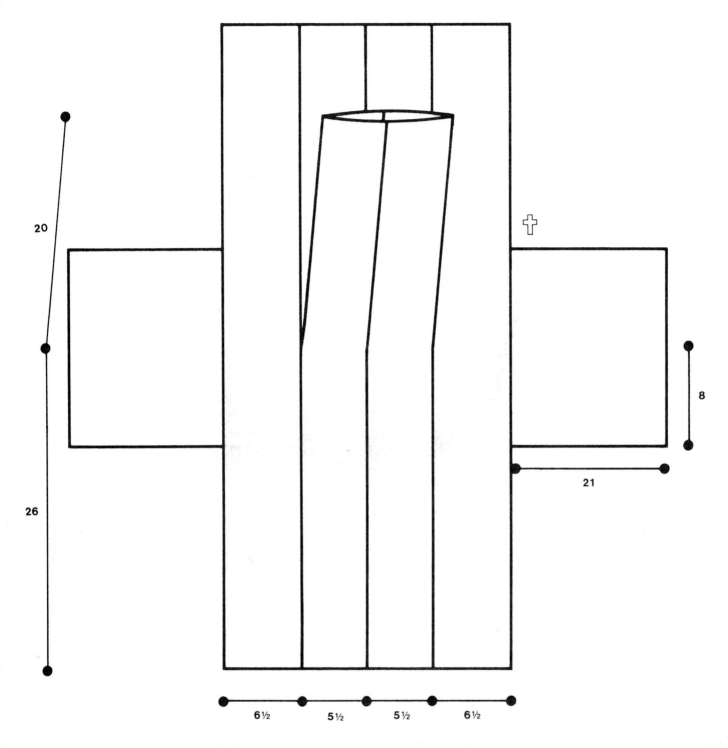

To make a long hood, crochet rectangles 1 through 4 extra long.

Materials: Heavy weight Irish Donegal (4 oz skns): 10 brown. Total Yardage: 2000. Hook: Size G. Gauge: 7 dcr = 2". Stitch: Dcr. Size: 5'6", 34-24-34. A long tube such as this can be folded several times to make a big turtleneck or pulled up and folded or rolled to make a cuffed hood. When choosing a yarn for this neck style make sure it is not too thick and will feel good against the skin. *Lesson 2* explains how to make a pullover with a long hood.

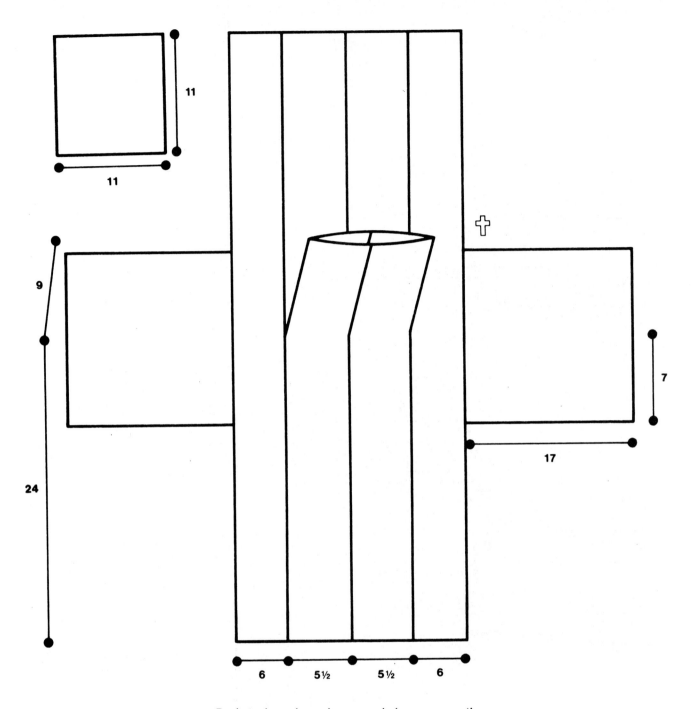

Pockets, in various shapes and sizes, are another way
to embellish the modular pullover.

Materials: Scheepjes Natuurwol (50 gram skns): 8 each of dark brown and
medium brown. Total Yardage: 1160 yards of each color. Hook: Size H. Gauge: 7
scr = 2". Stitch: Scr. Size: 5'6", 34-24-34. Pattern: Alternate 2 rows of each color.
The section *About Stitches and Detailing* shows you how to carry the yarns from
stripe to stripe. Work center pockets from the center out just as in rectangles 1 and
2 so the direction of the ridges will match on both sides of the center chain. All
other pockets are plain rectangles. For both types, work a chain to desired length.
Then work to desired width. Whipstitch the finished pocket into place.

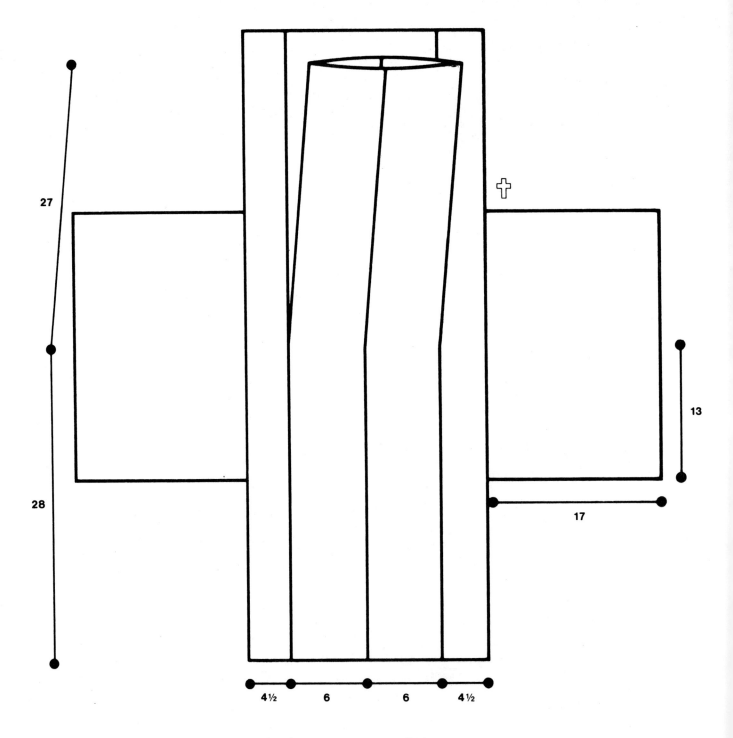

Cuffs—narrow or wide, folded or rolled—are an easy way
to alter the modular pullover.

Materials: Light weight Wool (2 oz skns): 14 ivory. Total Yardage: 1925. Hook:
Size E. Gauge: 11 dcr = 2″. Stitch: Dcr. Size: 5′6″, 34-24-34. An extra long tube
folded or rolled makes a pleasing sculptural form to arrange in various ways
around the face or neck. When making a tube this long, work in a lightweight yarn
or the cuff will be too thick to fit under the chain. To make cuffs for the sleeves, just
work them extra long.

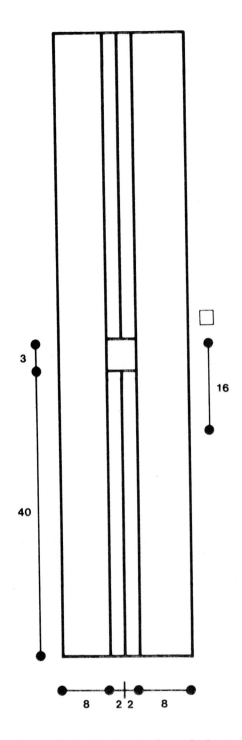

Six rectangles worked extra long make a sleek, streamlined tunic.

Materials: Light weight Wool (2 oz skns): 10 forest brown. Total Yardage: 2750. Hook: Size E. Gauge: 11 dcr = 2". Stitch: Dcr. Size: 5'6", 34-24-34. The photographs here, and in the *How to Work on Your Own* section, show how versatile the modular pullover crocheted tube is when it is worked vertically in the ridge stitch. Besides hanging well when it is worn straight, the fabric is so flexible that the garment—in any length, from sweater to ankle-length caftan—can be tied or bloused in various ways to create different effects.

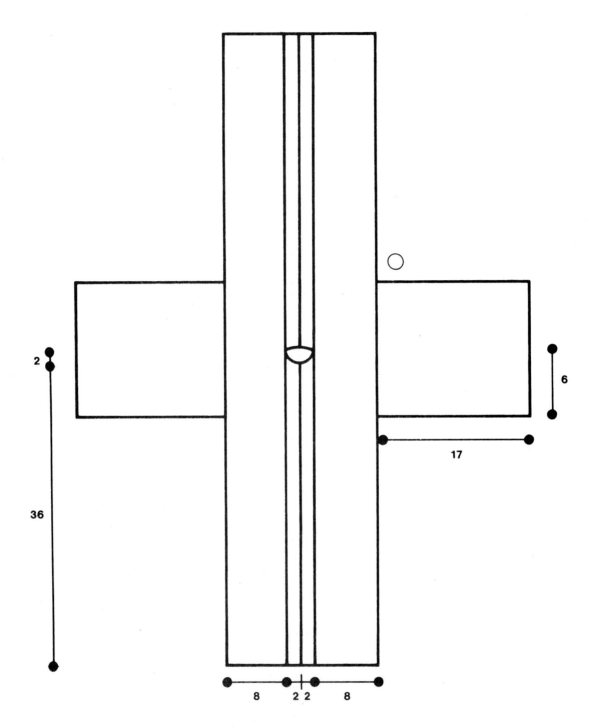

2

36

6

17

8   2 2   8

A plain knitting worsted worked in the dcr stitch
makes a dress that is comfortable, practical, and quick to make.

Materials: Knitting Worsted (4 oz skns): 8 dark brown. Total Yardage: 2260. Hook:
Size G. Gauge: 4 dcr = 1″. Stitch: Dcr. Size: 5′6″, 34-24-34. A basic shape such
as this one transcends the notorious whims of fashion, especially when worked in
a neutral color and a plain yarn. The easygoing, casual look is further reinforced
by working the fabric in the classic ridge stitch. Garments this plain can accom-
modate all sorts of accessories: scarves, stoles, long vests, among others. *See*
page 88, left.

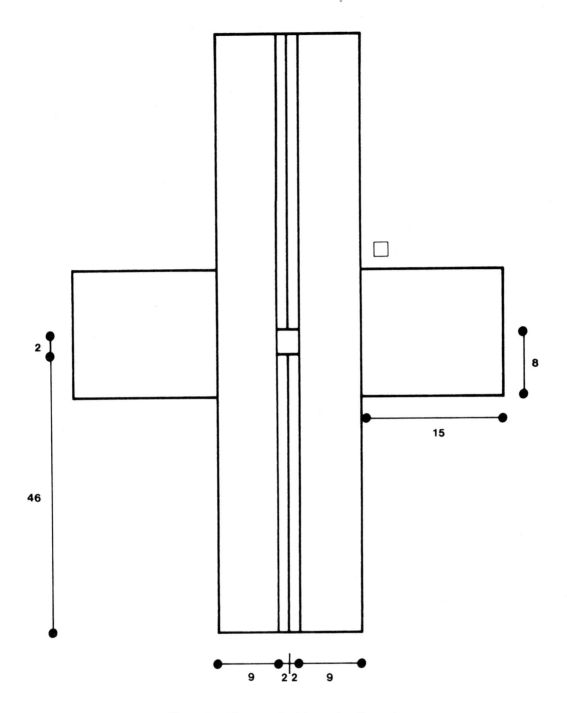

2

46

8

15

9   2 2   9

Alternate stripes worked in contrasting colors
create strong bold patterns for this modular pullover.

Materials: Alpacka (3.5 oz skns): 4 each of dark brown and medium brown. Total
Yardage: 1760 yards of each color. Hook: Size E. Gauge: 9 dcr = 2". Stitch: Dcr.
Size: 5'7", 34-24-34. When you alternate one row each of two colors, one color
will predominate because of the way the stitches fall. In this pullover, the body of
the garment shows one side of the fabric; the rolled up sleeves and scarf show the
other. Take advantage of this characteristic by putting the fabric together in different ways. The section *About Stitches and Detailing* tells how to make the scarf.
See page 88, right.

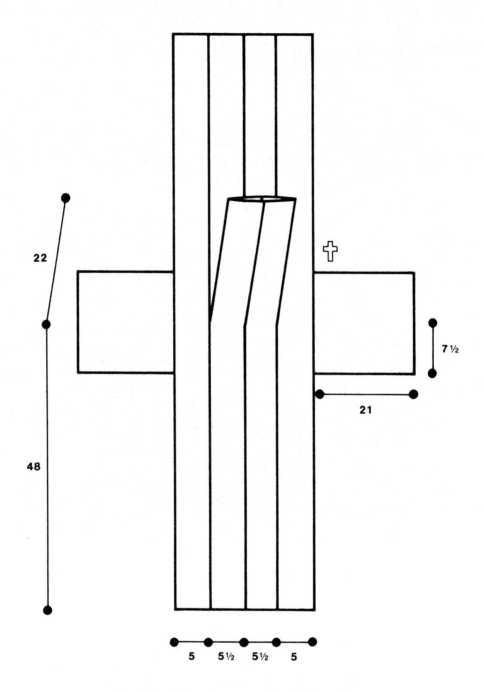

22

7½

48

21

5 5½ 5½ 5

Consider stripes—narrow, wide, bold, subtle,
allover patterns, at the edges, alternate—the possibilities are endless.

Materials: 3 ply Indiecita Alpaca (50 gram skns): 10 (A) dark brown, 5 each of (B)
medium brown, (C) light brown, 3 (D) camel. Total Yardage: A—1750, B,C—875
each, D—525. Hook: Size F. Gauge: 6 dcr = 1". Stitches: Dcr, scr. Size: 5'6",
34-24-34. In this coat-dress, stripes in closely related colors create striking linear
patterns as they wrap around the body. Rectangles 1 through 4: Work 1 row A in
the dcr. Then repeat throughout in the dcr, 2 rows each of B,C,D,A. Rectangles 5
and 6: Repeat throughout in the dcr, 1 row each of C,B,C,A. Rectangles 7 and 8:
Repeat throughout, 2 rows of C in the dcr, 2 rows of B in the scr, 2 rows of C in the
dcr, 2 rows of A in the scr. *See* page 89, left.

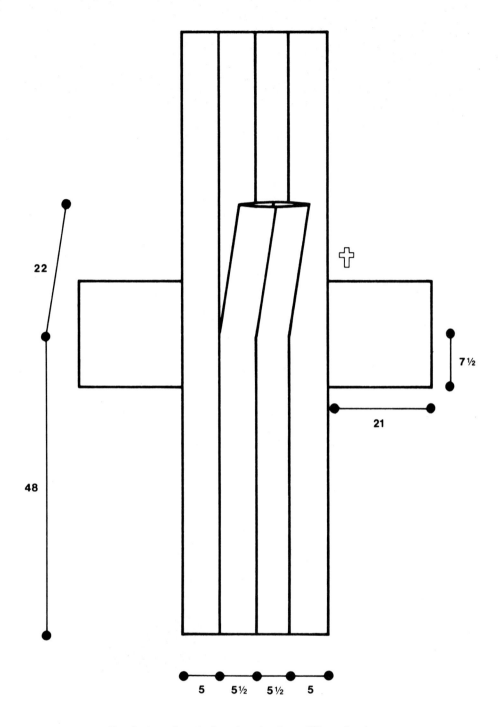

Crochet each set of rectangles in a different color.

Materials: Roma (3.5 oz skns): 5 (A) dark brown, 3 each of (B) medium brown and (C) light brown. Yardage: A—1750, B,C—1050. Hook: Size F. Gauge: 9 dcr = 2". Stitch: Dcr. Size: 5'6", 34-24-34. Color—alone or in combination—creates different moods and effects for the modular pullover. Bright primary colors are strong and vivid, soft pastels are romantic, the beige tones are neutral. Colors can be combined in any number of ways; for instance, you can make the sleeves or the cuffs a different color, or edge each rectangle in a bright color band, or use various stripe patterns. *See* page 89, right.

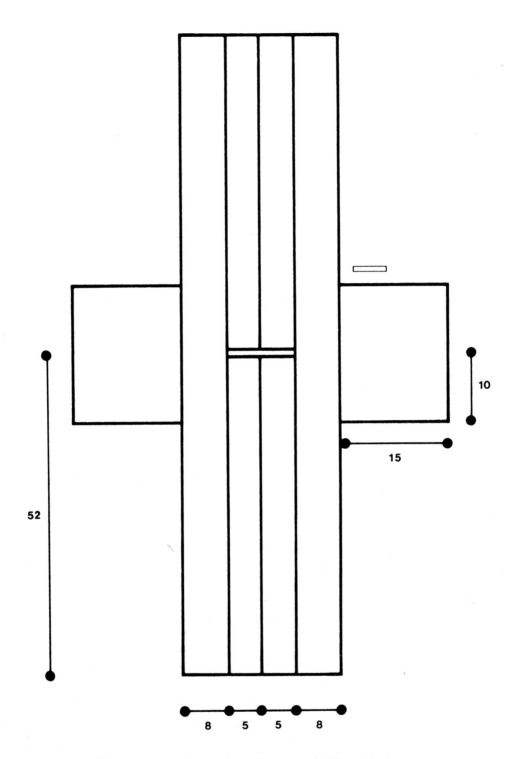

Stripes can also be crocheted in yarns of different textures.

Materials: Melody (1 oz skns): 17 black, Alpacka (3.5 oz skns): 4 brown. Total Yardage: 1760 yards of each color. Hook: Size F. Gauge: 9 dcr = 2″. Stitch: Dcr. Size: 5′7″, 34-24-34. Crochet the rectangles long and wide to make a loose-flowing caftan. Wear it straight or pull it up and blouse it to create other effects. To make the light and airy fabric, crochet loosely, alternating the stripes in a fluffy mohair blend and a heather-toned wool and alpaca blend.

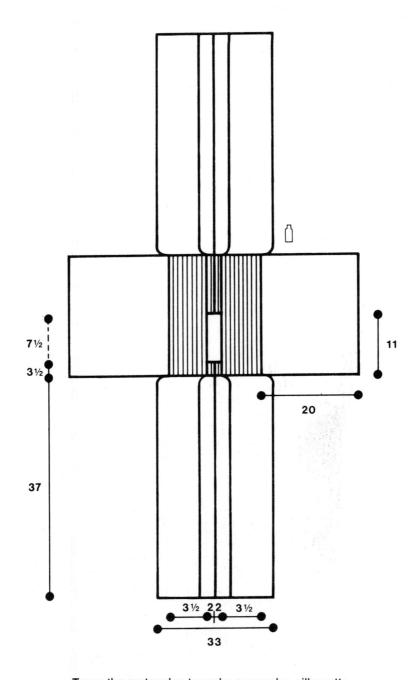

<table>
</table>

7½

3½

11

37

20

3½ 2 2 3½

33

Taper the rectangles to make a complex silhouette.

Materials: Feu d'Artifice (20 gram balls): 11 each of black and silver. Belangor Angora (10 gram balls) 25 black. El Molino Rayon Floss, 2 tubes wine. Total Yardage: 1485 yards of black and silver, 825 yards of angora, 115 yards of rayon. Hooks: Sizes E, G. Gauge: 6 dcr = 1″. Sleeves: 4 dcr = 1″. Stitches: Scr, dcr. Size: 5′6″, 34-24-34. The smocked silhouette and the choice of yarns and colors give this modular pullover a simple elegance. With 2 strands of the rayon floss and an E hook, make the center chain, work row 1 in the single crochet stitch. Row 2: Crocheting the angora tightly, work the skirt in the dcr, and the bodice in the scr. Next Rows: Alternating 1 row each of the silver, then black metallic, work one scr in each scr, one dcr in each dcr. Sleeves—Row 1: With the angora and a G hook work one dcr in *every other* stitch. Next Rows: One dcr in each dcr.

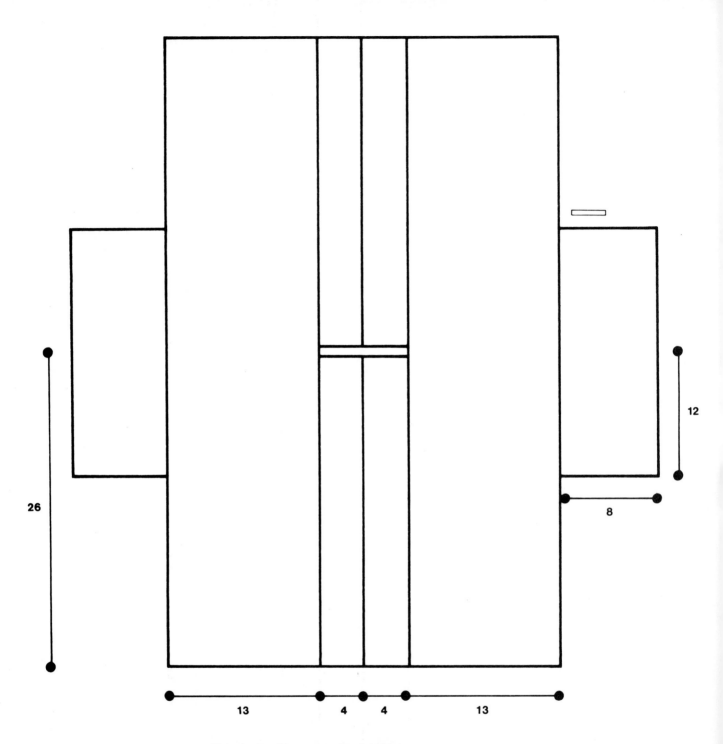

26

12

8

13   4   4   13

Extremely wide rectangles, worked in a very bulky yarn,
make a pullover with an unusual look and silhouette.

Materials: 3 cut Cotton Chenille (4 oz skns): 9 ivory. Total Yardage: 540. Hook:
Size Q. Gauge: 6 scr = 5″. Stitch: Scr. Size: 5′7″, 34-24-34. Even though it is extra
wide, this big, soft, floppy top was crocheted in an afternoon. So, if you never
seem to be able to finish a project, want quick results, or need a sweater in a
hurry, choose one of the bulky yarns and work it up with an extra big hook. Neck
Trim: On the wrong side of the fabric, work 1 row of scr.

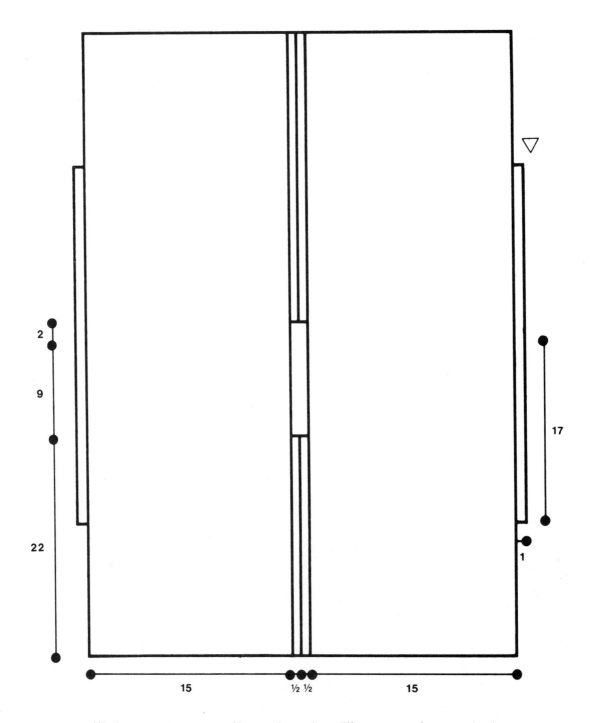

Work a repeat pattern making each row in a different type of yarn and color.

Materials: 350 yards of each type yarn: Cotillion: (A) black-silver and Feu d'Artifice: (B) brown-silver. Alpacka: (C) dark brown and (D) medium brown. Arianne: (E) rust. 3 ply Indiecita Alpaca: (F) dark brown, (G) medium brown, (H) blonde. El Molino Rayon Floss: 10 tubes of (I) black, 5 tubes each of (J) wine, (K) silver. Hook: Size E. Gauge: 11 dcr = 2". Stitch: Dcr. Size: 5'6", 34-24-34. Pattern: Repeat throughout 1 row each of A and C; 1 row of 1 strand each of I and J held together; 1 row each of H,B,F,E,D; 1 row of 1 strand each of I and K held together; and 1 row of G.

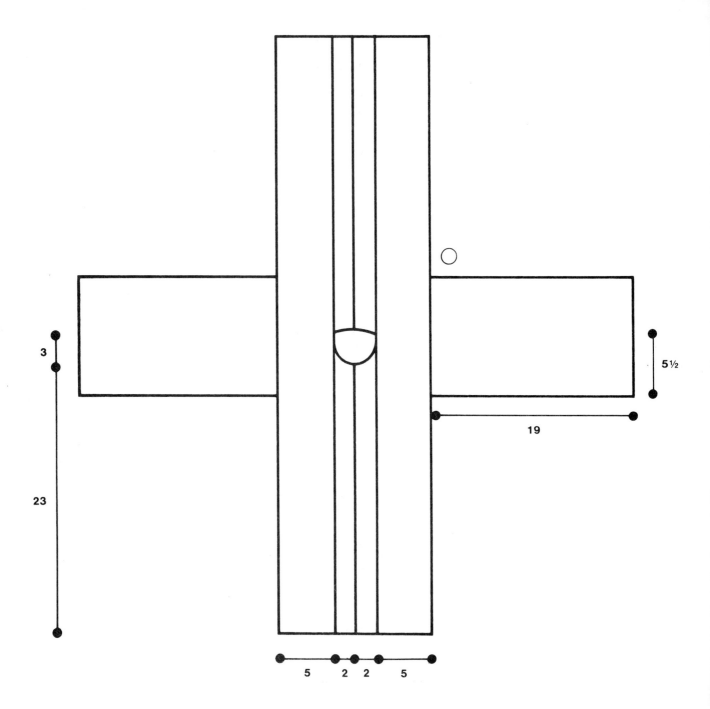

Narrow rectangles, worked in a light weight yarn,
make a pullover that hugs the body.

Materials: Roma (3.5 oz skns): 4 of color 135. Total Yardage: 1400. Hook: Size F.
Gauge: 9 hdcr = 2″. Stitch: Hdcr. Size: 5′6″, 34-24-34. Keep in mind that narrow
rectangles stretch to fit the body when the garment is put on. When working the
center rectangles 1 through 4, make them narrower than usual. If they are worked
too wide, you may find the neck opening is wider than desired when the garment is
stretched. To get a good fit, work the rectangles simultaneously and try them on
as you add the rows. Tug at them a bit to get an idea how they will look and fit
when stretched around the body. *See* page 102, left.

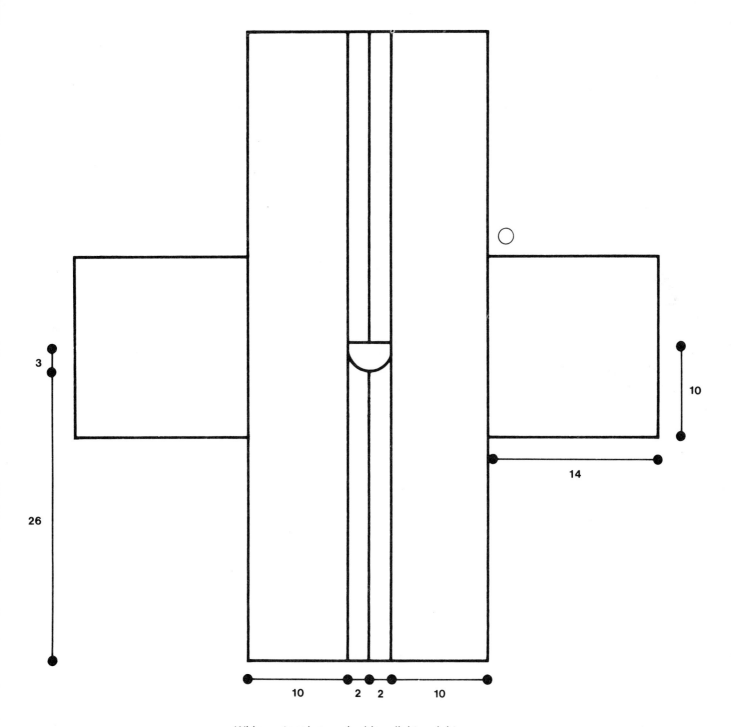

Wide rectangles worked in a light weight yarn
make a pullover that hangs loose and free.

Materials: Alpacka (3.5 oz skns): 5 dark brown. Total Yardage: 2400. Hook: Size
E. Gauge: 5 dcr = 1″. Stitch: Dcr. Size: 5′7″, 34-24-34. When the body of
the pullover is worked wider than 18 inches the fabric starts to hang loose from the
body, adding new dimensions to the modular shape, as it falls into soft, graceful
folds. The wide sleeves add even more drama to this sophisticated silhouette.
Neck Trim: On right side, crochet 1 row of scr around the entire edge. *See* page
102, right.

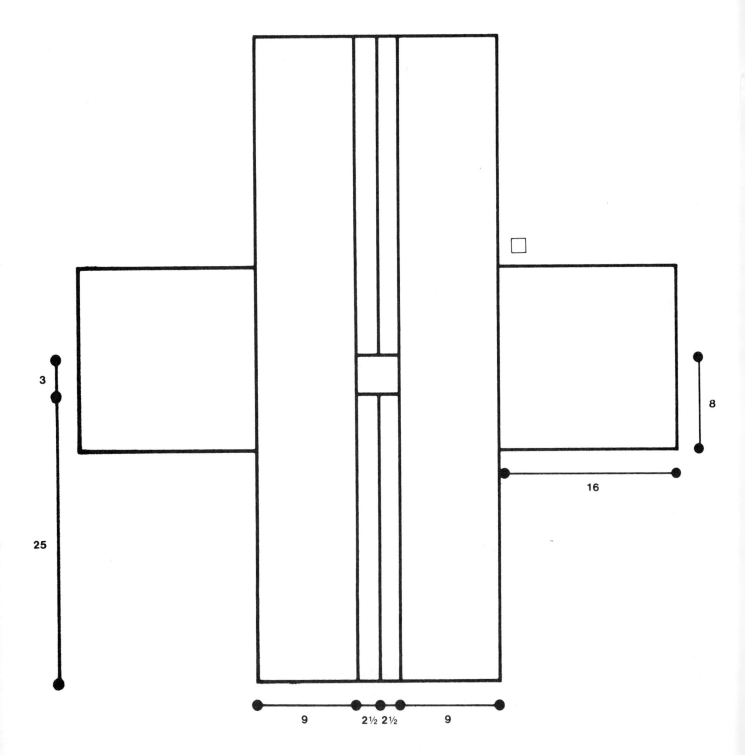

Bulky yarn works up quickly and makes a fabric that is thick and warm.

Materials: Lopi (100 gram skns): 10 white. Total Yardage: 1190. Hook: Size J. Gauge: 3 hdcr = 1". Stitch: Hdcr. Size: 5'6", 34-24-34. When choosing a stitch keep in mind that in the same yarn each stitch will make a different weight fabric. The half double crochet ridge stitch makes a medium weight fabric with medium width ridges and is further characterized by the interlocking loops along the tops of the ridges. *See* page 103, left.

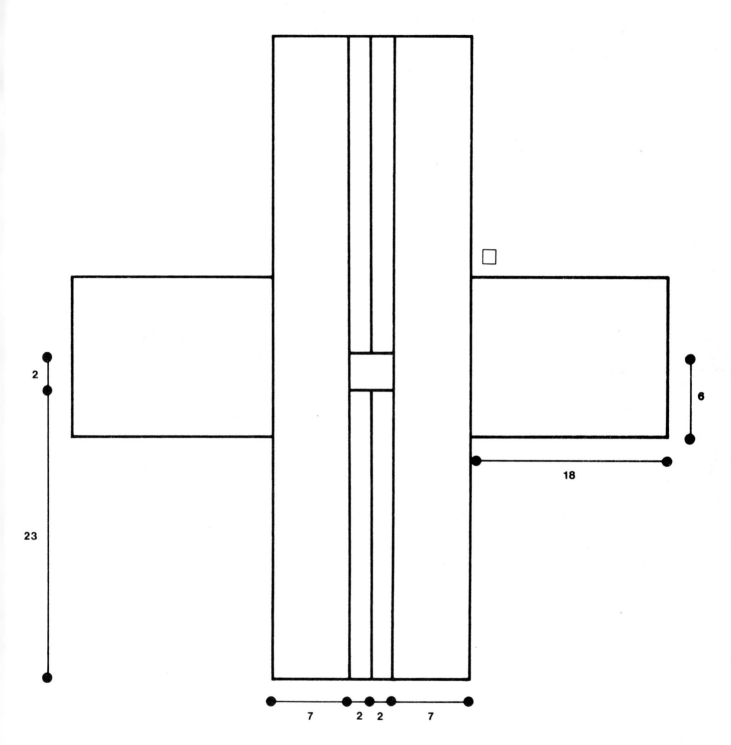

Working the same yarn in a different stitch
gives the pullover a completely different look.

Materials: Lopi (100 gram skns): 8 light brown. Total Yardage: 960. Hook: Size J.
Gauge: 3 scr = 1″. Stitch: Scr. Size 34-24-34. This pullover is worked in the single
crochet ridge stitch. By comparison note that the fabric is thicker, with ridges that
are deeper and narrower. In the same yarn, the double crochet ridge stitch,
because it is the longest and thinnest stitch, makes the lightest weight fabric with
the widest ridges. See page 103, right.

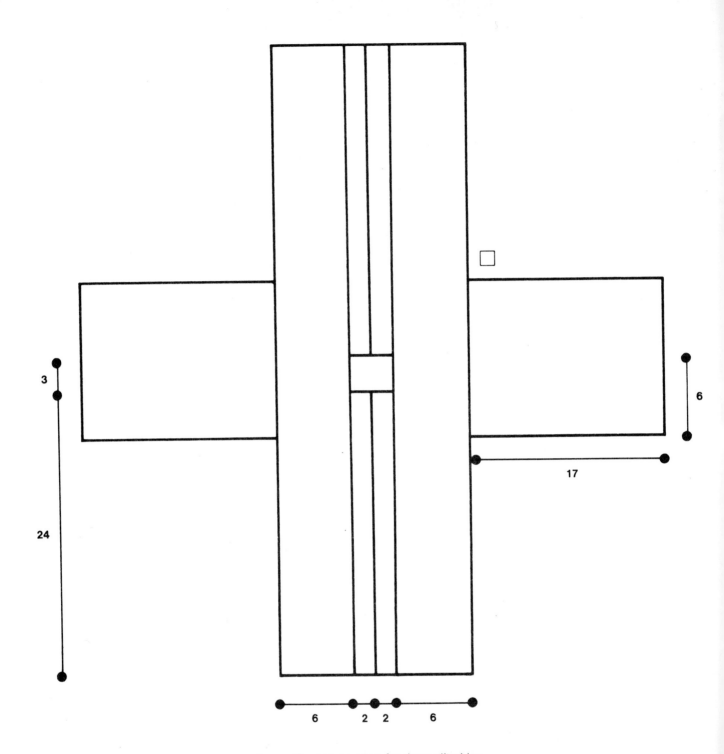

Leave the seams open for deep slit sides,
then decorate the modular pullover with wrapped, tied, and twisted scarves.

Materials: Andes Alpaca (4 oz. skns): 7 blonde. Scarves: 1 skein of each color for
each scarf. Total Yardage: 1470. Hook: Size H. Gauge: 4 hdcr = 1″. Stitch: Hdcr.
Scarves: Scr, hdcr, dcr. Size: 5′6″, 34-24-34. Scarves are simply rectangles which
can be made in any length, width, stitch, or pattern. To crochet them, make a
chain the length of the scarf, then work from the center out just as with rectangles
1 and 2. The section *About Stitches and Detailing* tells you how to proceed.

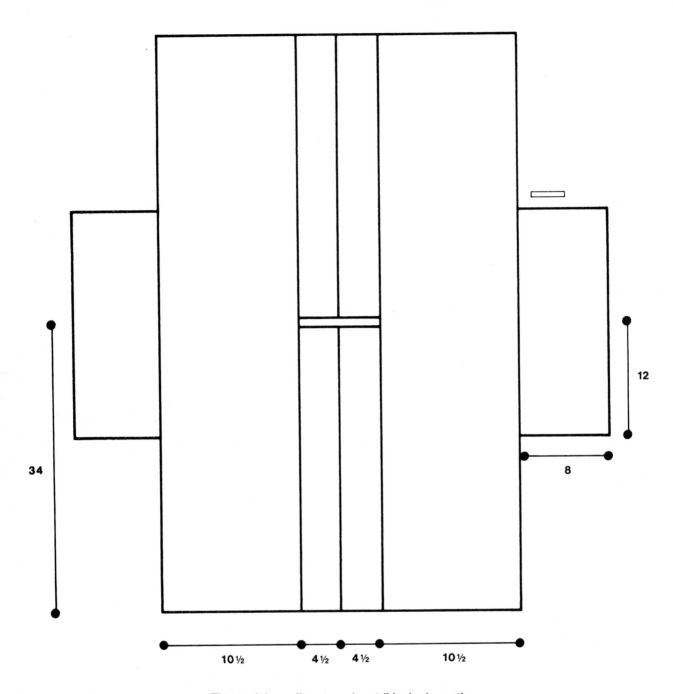

The modular pullover can be strikingly dramatic
as shown in this wide poncho of mixed yarns, colors, and textures.

Materials: Mirabella (2 oz skns): 8 black. Handspun Colombian Wool (4 oz skns);
24 ozs of various colors. 3 ply Indiecita Alpaca (50 gram skns); 1 each of black
and beige. Total Yardage: 3000 yards of mixed yarns. Hook: Size J. Gauge: 3 scr
= 1". Stitch: Scr. Size 5'7", 34-24-34. Mixing different yarns, colors, and stitches
is exciting but results in many end threads. For a variation, instead of crocheting
over the end threads, let them hang free as a decorative element. This not only
saves time but is a fine way to show off the colors and textures of an unusual
yarn. If there is not enough texture in the end threads when the garment is complete, add more fringes.

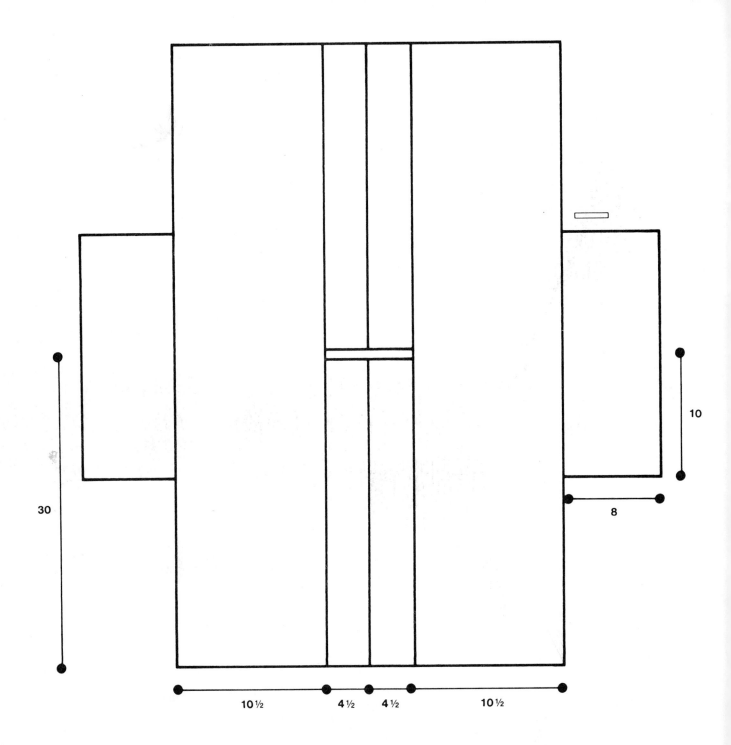

Enhance the modular pullover with soft jewelry made from silver crocheted cords.

Materials: Cotillion (30 gram skns): 22 black-silver. Cords: Feu d'Artifice (20 gram skns): 3 silver. Total Yardage: 2750. Cords: 405. Hook: Size F. Cords: Size H. Gauge: 6 dcr = 1″. Stitch: Dcr. Size: 5′6″, 34-24-34. Fabrics made from elaborate yarns are sophisticated and yet informal when worked into a simple shape with flowing lines. The silver in this particular yarn is echoed in the decorative soft jewelry that loops and ties in many ways. To make the round cords, work two strands held together; the section *About Stitches and Detailing* tells you how.

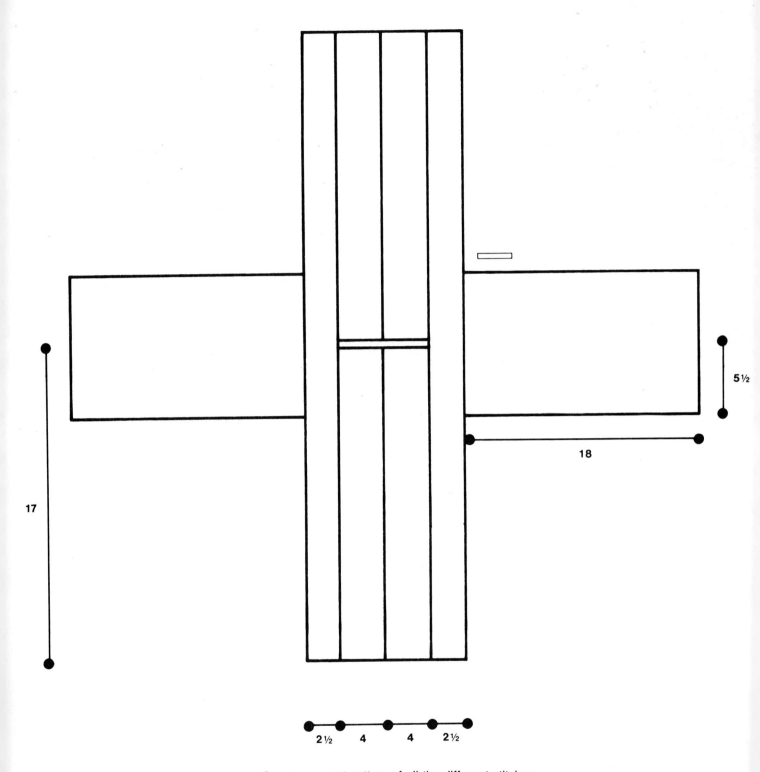

Create a repeat pattern of all the different stitches.

Materials: Classique (50 gram skns): 8 natural. Total Yardage: 1000. Hook: Size F. Stitches: Scr, hdcr, dcr. Size: 5'6", 34-24-34. Rectangles 1 through 4: To make this decorative fabric, work row 1 in the scr stitch. Next Rows: Repeat in order throughout the sweater, 2 rows hdcr, 6 rows scr, 4 rows dcr, 6 rows scr. *Lesson 2* explains how to make a boat neck.

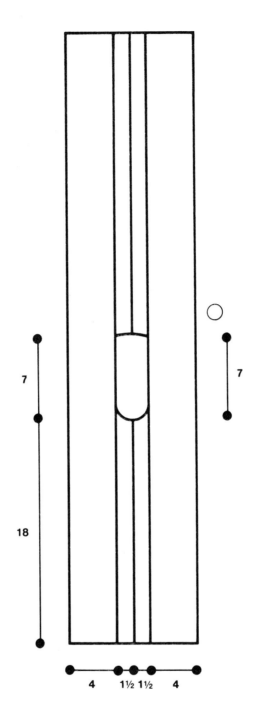

7

7

18

4   1½ 1½   4

When worked in a suitable yarn the same six rectangles
of the skinny ribbed tank top also make a long narrow vest.

Materials: 3 ply Indiecita Alpaca (50 gram skns): 2 each of dark brown and camel.
Total Yardage: 110 yards of each color. Hook: Size J. Gauge: 3 scr = 1″. Stitch:
Scr. Size: 5′6″, 34-24-34. To make an informal fabric with a subtle overall pattern,
choose a furry alpaca in two muted colors and work the two strands held together
throughout. If you want to round the neck opening as we have done, follow the
instructions for the tank top. *Lesson 2* tells how to round the neck opening for
other weight yarns. *See* page 116, left.

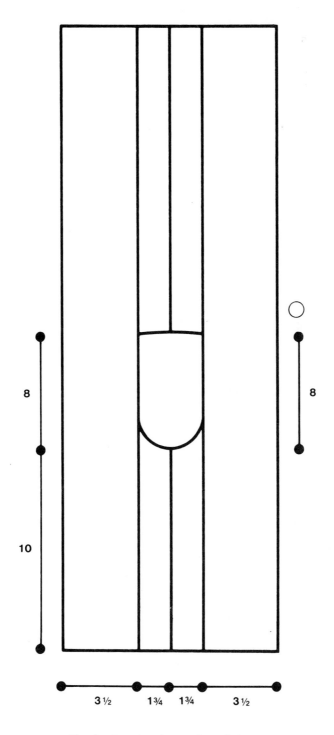

Six short rectangles make a little vest.

Materials: 3 ply Indiecita Alpaca (50 gram skns): 2 each of dark brown and beige. Total Yardage: 110 of each color. Hook: Size J. Gauge: 3 dcr = 1″. Stitches: Alternate 1 row scr, 1 row dcr. For this vest 2 strands of alpaca in contrasting colors are worked held together. The resulting fabric, with its strong irregular pattern, looks like the coat of an exotic animal. Neck Trim: On right side of fabric work 2 rows of scr. To turn this garment into a sweater, add sleeves, short or long, and consider cuffs, big or little. *See* page 116, right.

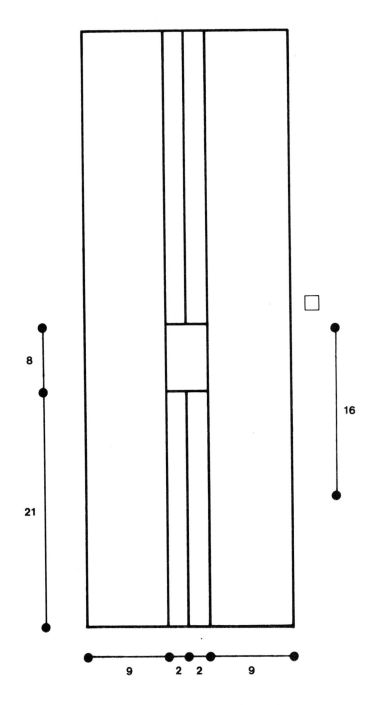

Rectangles are decorative and complex
when mixed yarns, colors, and stitches are worked in random patterns.

Crochet stitches in different colors and textures, work a row in 4, 7, 10 different colors. Use as many yarns as you want; work a single strand or combine 2 or more, however your fancy strikes you. When adding combined yarns, remember to keep the thicknesses approximately the same as that of the single yarns so the gauge and fabric will be *about* the same throughout. A little variation in the thicknesses, however, won't cause any problems. We have used yarns such as variegated brushed wools, shiny rayons, metallics, matte cottons, thick-and-thin handspun wools, and multicolored tweeds. *See* page 117, left.

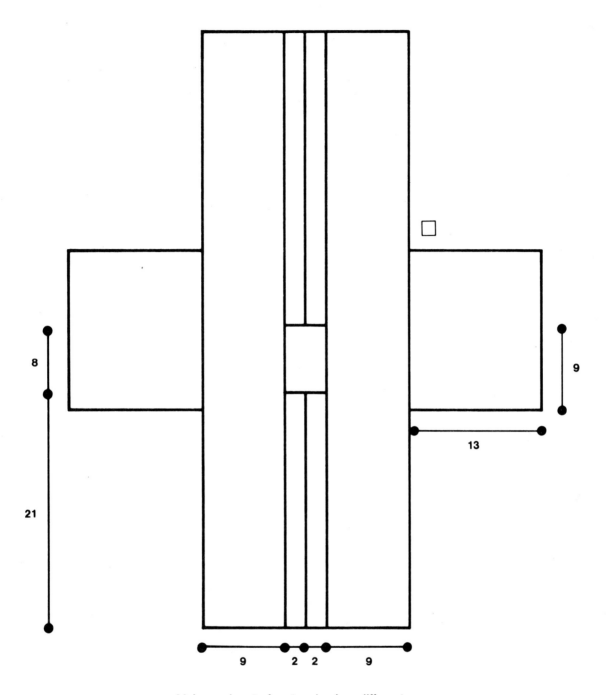

Make each set of rectangles in a different yarn.

Add even more pattern and texture by mixing the colors and stitches of each yarn in various ways throughout. Hook: Size J. Rectangles 1 through 4 are crocheted in 4 colors of Sugar 'n Cream, Cotton, 125 yards each. Rectangles 5 and 6 are crocheted in Handspun Colombian Sheepswool, roughspun wool, 750 yards. Rectangles 7 and 8 are crocheted in Parisian Cotton, 952 yards café and 476 yards beige. Work 2 strands of café and 1 of beige held together in the dcr stitch to make a tweed. Trim: For a change, crochet an extra large border around the bottom of the garment. With 2 strands of the Sugar 'n Cream cotton held together, attach the yarn and work 2 rows of scr, then work 2 rows of dcr. *See* page 117, right.

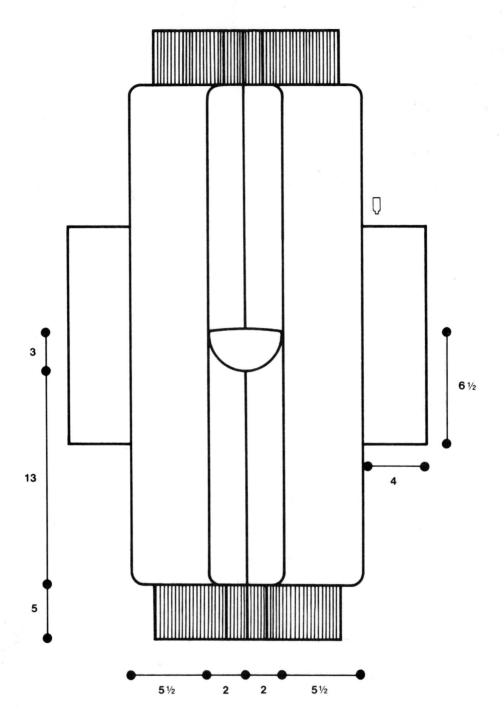

3

6½

13

4

5

5½   2   2   5½

Tapered rectangles worn straight make a shaped pullover of classic proportions.

Materials: Knitting Worsted (4 oz skns): 3 light brown. Total Yardage: 780. Hook: Size G. Gauge: 4 hdcr = 1″. Stitches: Scr, hdcr. Size: 5′6″, 34-24-34. When the scr and the hdcr are worked in the same row, and the garment is worn straight rather than being pulled up and bloused, the slight taper at the bottom makes the pullover a conventionally shaped sweater. To work two different stitches in the same row, follow the instructions for the chenille vest (previous pattern) from row 1. Sleeve Trim: End with a few rows of the scr stitch if desired. For a snugger fit, try working it on a smaller size hook.

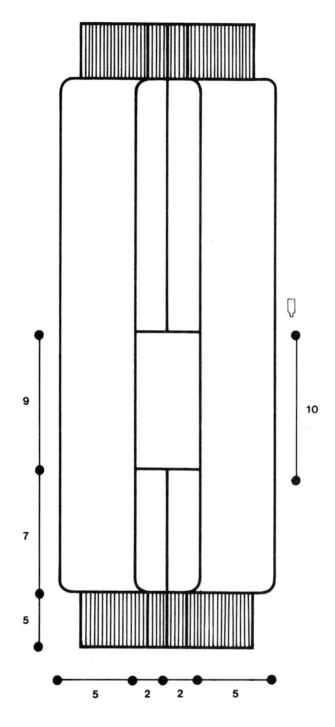

Note how the same shape is totally transformed when worked in different yarns.

Materials: Vest 1: Handspun Colombian Sheepswool (4 oz. skns): 3 natural. Hook: Size J. Gauge: 3 hdcr = 1″. Vest 2: Dji Dji Brushed Wool (125 yard skns): 3 mixed browns. Hook: Size J. Gauge: 3 hdcr = 1″. Six short rectangles, tapered at the bottom and worn straight, make a little, shaped vest. The body is worked in the hdcr stitch. The waistband is worked in the scr stitch. To work two different stitches in the same row, follow the instructions for the chenille vest (see page 128) from row 1.

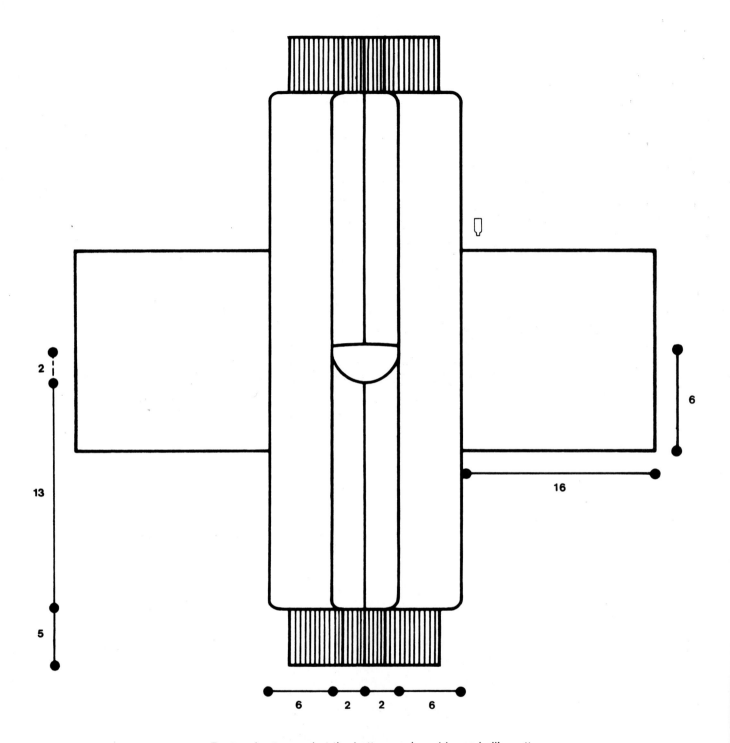

Rectangles tapered at the bottom make a bloused silhouette.

Materials: Belangor Angora (10 gram balls): 34 chestnut. Total Yardage: 1122 yards. Hook: Size G. Gauge: 4 hdcr = 1″. Stitches: Scr, hdcr. Size: 5′6″, 34-24-34. Pattern: Work 1 scr in each scr. Work 1 hdcr in each hdcr. When the scr and hdcr are worked in the same row and the shorter stitch is at the bottom of the rectangles, the fabric is pulled in at the bottom of the rectangle to create a bloused silhouette. *Lesson 2* tells you how to read the diagram. The next diagram tells you how to taper the rectangles.

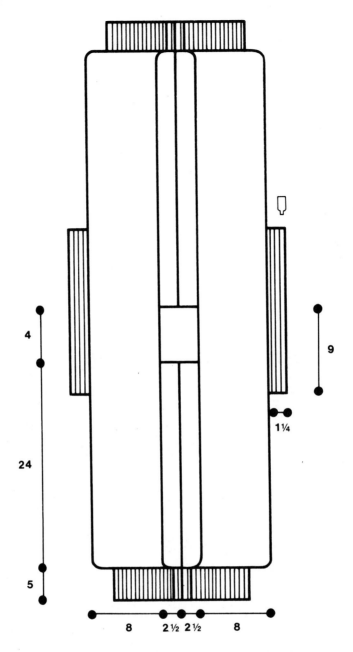

When 2 different stitches are worked in the same row,
how the stitches are apportioned determines where the blouse will fall.

Materials: Velourette Chenille (1 oz skns): 17 terre cuite. Total Yardage: 986. Hook: Size G. Gauge: 4 hdcr = 1″. Stitches: Scr, hdcr. Size: 5′6″, 34-24-34. Rectangle 1: The beginning center chain should include enough stitches for the body-hugging band (the shaded section), the body of the garment from top of band to neck edge and 4 extra inches for the overlap or blouse (the unshaded section). Row 1: Work the hdcr for the body of the garment and the overlap, then finish the row in the scr for the body-hugging band. Next Rows and Rectangle 2—Pattern: Work 1 scr in each scr; work 1 hdcr in each hdcr. Rectangle 3: Work center back chain. Work hdcr, *then finish the row in the same amount of scr as the front.* Next Rows: Work 1 scr in each scr, work 1 hdcr in each hdcr throughout. Sleeves: For this vest they are worked in the scr.

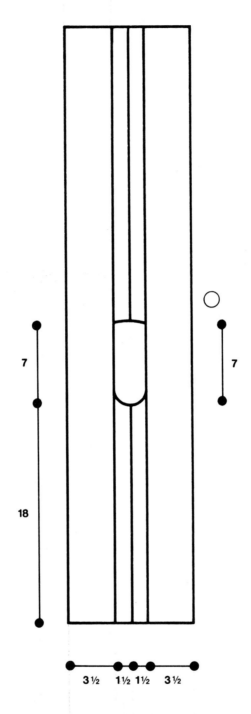

Six rectangles worked long and narrow
make a skinny ribbed tank top that stretches to fit the body.

Materials: Sugar 'n Cream (2 oz skns): 5 light brown. Total Yardage: 625. Hook: Size H. Gauge: 4 scr = 1″. Stitch: Scr. Size: 5′6″, 34-24-34. To make the tank top in this yarn rectangles 1 through 4 are each 7 rows wide. Rectangles 1 and 2: To round the neck, increase 1 stitch at the neck edge on rows 4, 6, and 7. Rectangles 3 and 4: Increase 1 stitch at neck edge on the last row of each rectangle. Rectangles 5 and 6: Add in the usual way. Neck Trim: On right side, work 1 row of scr. To round the neck opening for other weight yarns consult *Lesson 2.*

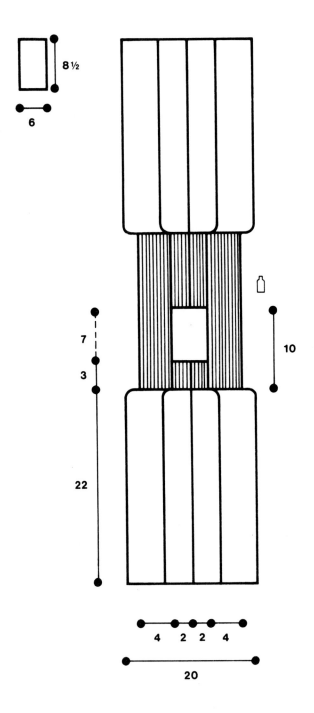

Work two different stitches in the same row to make the smocked silhouette.

Materials: Medium weight common hardware store string: 12 natural. Total Yardage: 1500. Hook: Size H. Gauge: 4 scr = 1″. Stitches: Scr, hdcr. Size: 5′6″, 34-24-34. Rectangle 1—Front: Work the beginning center chain to desired length. Row 1: Starting with scr, work desired number of stitches for the bodice (narrow part of garment), then switch to hdcr and finish the row in the longer stitch to make the skirt (wider part of garment). Next Rows—Pattern: Work 1 scr in each scr. Work 1 hdcr in each hdcr. Rectangle 3: Work center back chain. Work in scr, *then finish the row in the same amount of hdcr as the front.* Then work 1 scr in each scr, work 1 hdcr in each hdcr throughout.

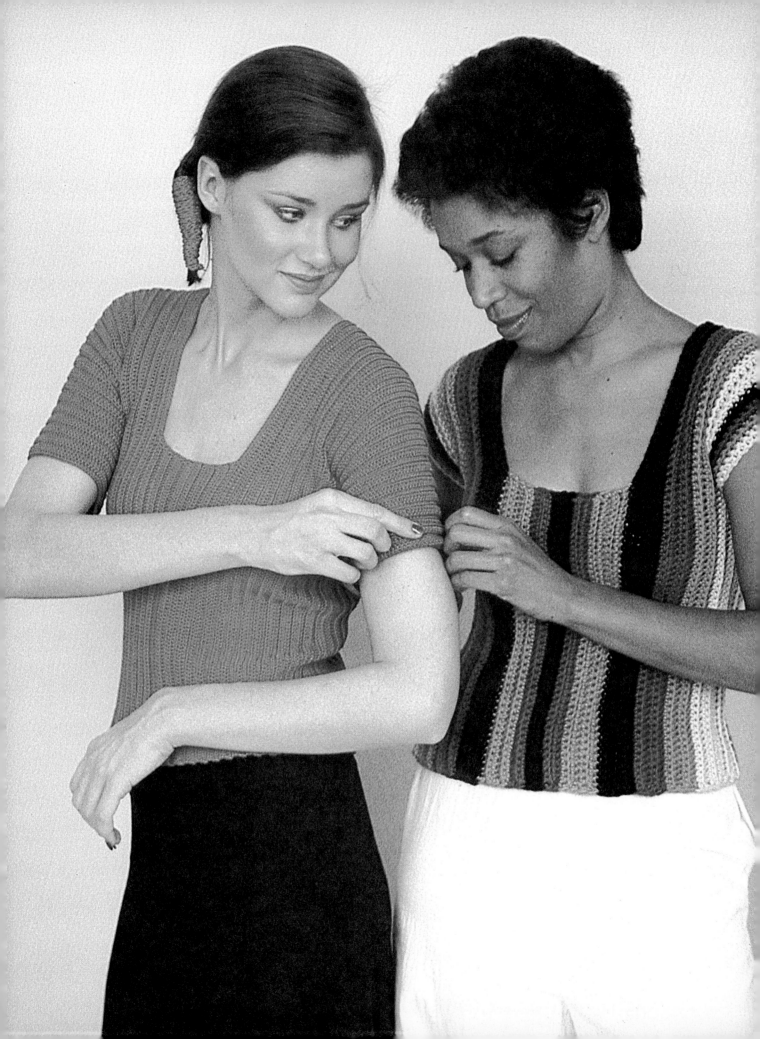

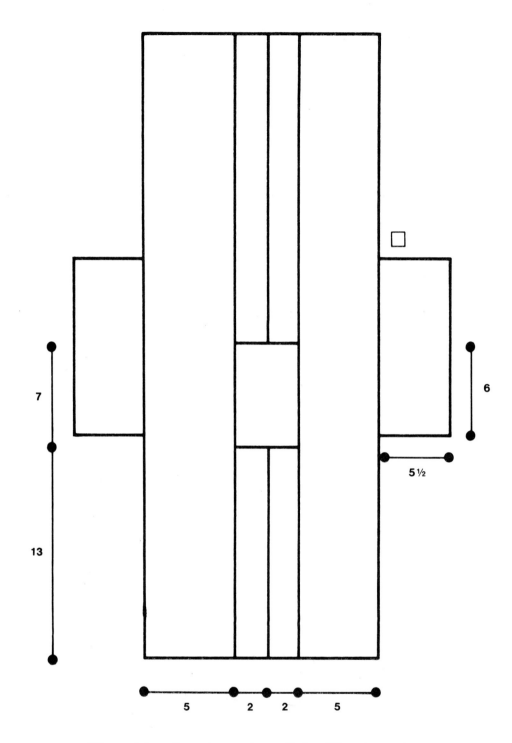

The modular pullover is easy to modify for different occasions.

Materials: Parisian Cotton (1 oz balls): 11 brique. Total Yardage: 1320. Hook: Size 0. Gauge: 6 dcr = 1". Stitch: Dcr. Size: 5'7", 34-24-34. Except for the sleeves, which are a bit longer, this shape is the same as the next top in the ombré colors. Note how formal the modular pullover becomes when worked in a soft lustered cotton and a single color. To alter the pullover in yet another way and to make it a warmer garment, choose a heathery tweed, and make the neck opening higher and the sleeves even longer for short folded cuffs. *See* page 134, left.

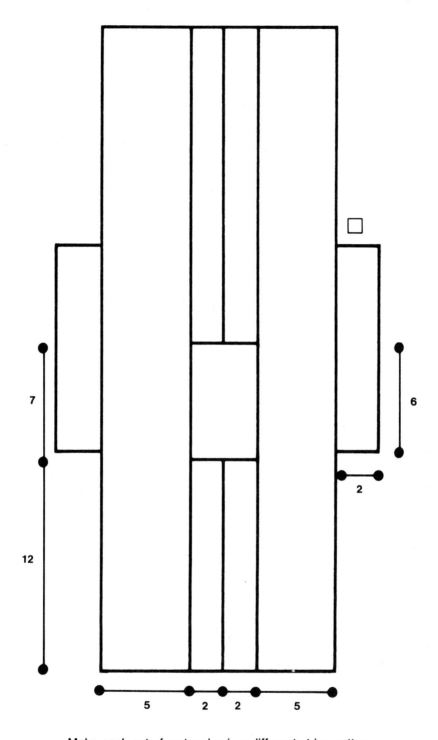

Make each set of rectangles in a different stripe pattern.

Materials: Sugar 'n Cream (2 oz balls): 2 each of black, rust, light brown, beige.
Total Yardage: 250 of each color. Hook: Size H. Gauge: 4 scr = 1". Stitch: Scr.
Size: 5'6", 34-24-34. For a rhythmic, undulating pattern, arrange the colors so
they go from dark to light. Rectangles 1 through 4: 1 row black, 2 rows rust, 4 rows
light brown. Rectangles 5 through 6: 4 rows each of black, rust, light brown, beige.
Rectangles 7 through 8: 2 rows each of black, rust, light brown, beige. See page
134, right.

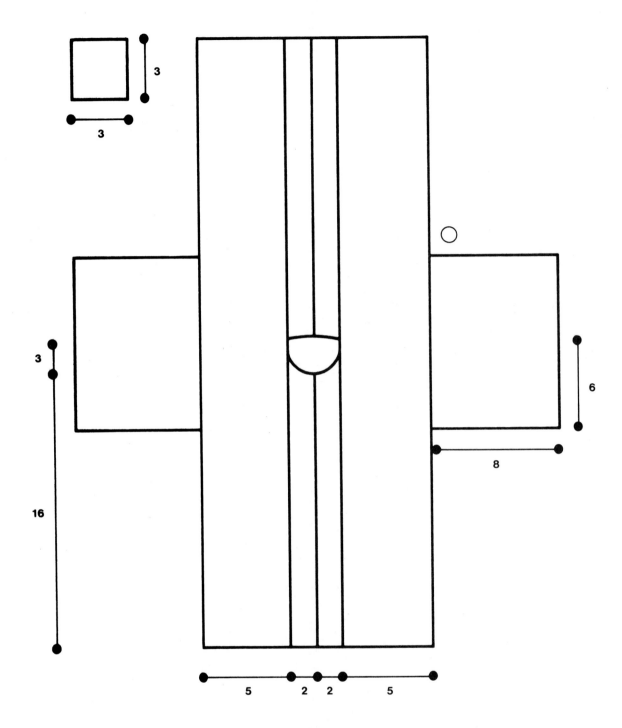

Round the neck and add big roll-up cuffs and two patch pockets
to make a casual T-shirt.

Materials: Blue Label Bedspread Cotton (400 yard skns): 8 skeins ivory. Total Yardage: 3200. Hook: Size J. Gauge: 7 scr = 2″. Stitch: Scr. Size: 5′6″, 34-24-34. If you want a bulky look for your T-shirt, work the pullover in one thick strand or combine several thin strands (we used four) as we have done. Then make big stitches by working the yarn loosely on a big hook. *Lesson 2* explains how to round the neck. Neck Edging: Working on wrong side, loosely crochet 1 row of scr. *See* page 135, left.

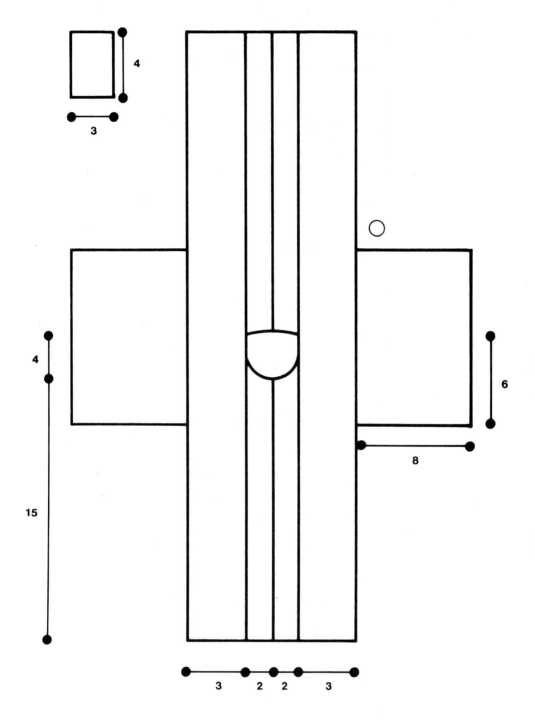

Working with mixed yarns is another way
to vary the fabric for the modular pullover.

Materials: El Molino Rayon Floss (25 gram tubes): 5 each of black, rust, ivory, gray, ocher. Total Yardage: 575 yards of each color. Hook: Size J. Gauge: 2 scr = 1″ Stitch: Scr. Size: 5′6″, 34-24-34. We have combined five shiny rayons in contrasting colors to make a sleek and stretchy fabric that expands to fit the body. Note in the diagram how narrow the rectangles are. Neck Edging: Working on the wrong side of the fabric loosely crochet 1 row of scr. The section *About Yarn* tells you how to work with mixed yarns and rayon yarns. *See* page 135, right.

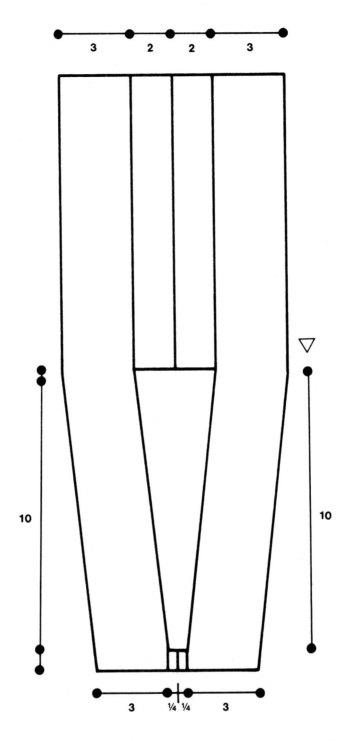

3   2   2   3

10   10

3   ¼ ¼   3

Make a V neck by working rectangles 1 and 2 only 1 row wide.

Materials: Sugar 'n Cream (2 oz skns): 1 each of black and beige. Total Yardage: 250. Hook: Size H. Gauge: 4 scr = 1″. Stitch: Scr. Size: 5′6″, 34-24-34. Pattern: Alternate 2 rows of each color. The halter is the only style where rectangles 3 and 4 are worked wider than rectangles 1 and 2. This is done in order to get a comfortable fit at the back of the neck. Join them together in the usual way, then add rectangles 5 and 6. Bottom Trim: Work 1 row sc around the end stitch of each row. Work 1 scr in each scr for the next two rows.

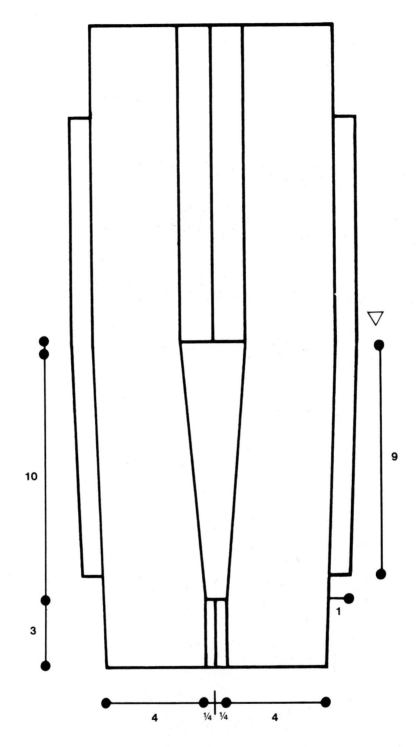

A fluffy yarn transforms the modular garment into a soft silhouette.

Materials: Belangor Angora (10 gram balls): 12 black. Total Yardage: 396. Hook: Size G. Gauge: 3 scr = 1". Stitch: Scr. Size: 5'6", 34-24-34. To soften the lines even more we have worked this halter with short, wide sleeves and added a long tie, looped in the center, to gather the fabric in. Observe that rectangles 3 and 4 are wider than rectangles 1 and 2. This is done in order to get a comfortable fit at the back of the neck.

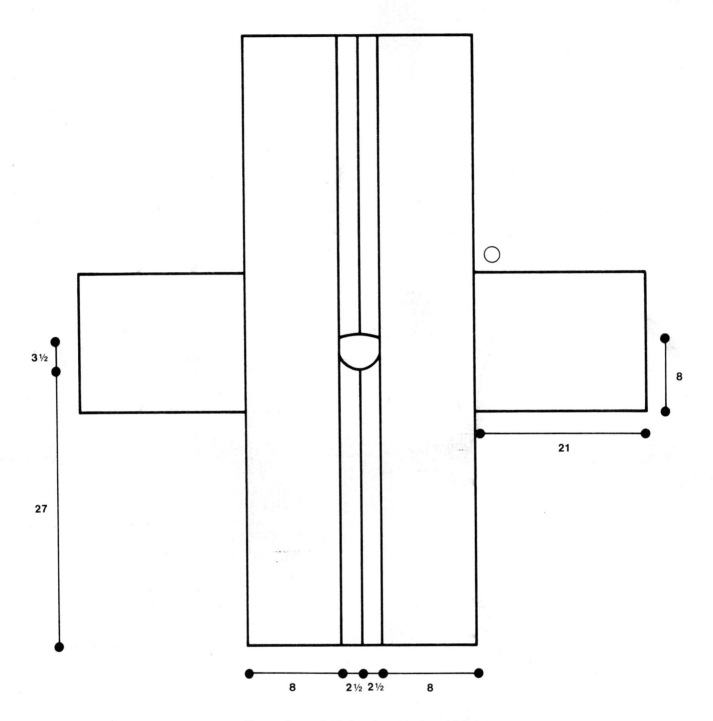

3½

8

27

21

8   2½ 2½   8

To crochet a richly hued and textured fabric
select a yarn that is spun from natural fibers.

Materials: Icelandic Homespun (50 gram skns): 15 dark brown. Total Yardage:
1785. Hook: Size H. Gauge: 7 scr = 2″. Stitch: Scr. Size: 6′, 38-32-36. The coat of
an animal is a rich blend of many subtle hues and tones, and yarns spun from
animal fibers are especially pleasing because they glow with color and depth.
Animal fibers also have special physical qualities. They may be kinky or extremely
long, very soft and silky or coarse. When crocheted, natural fibers make fabrics
that are fascinating in their variety and beauty.

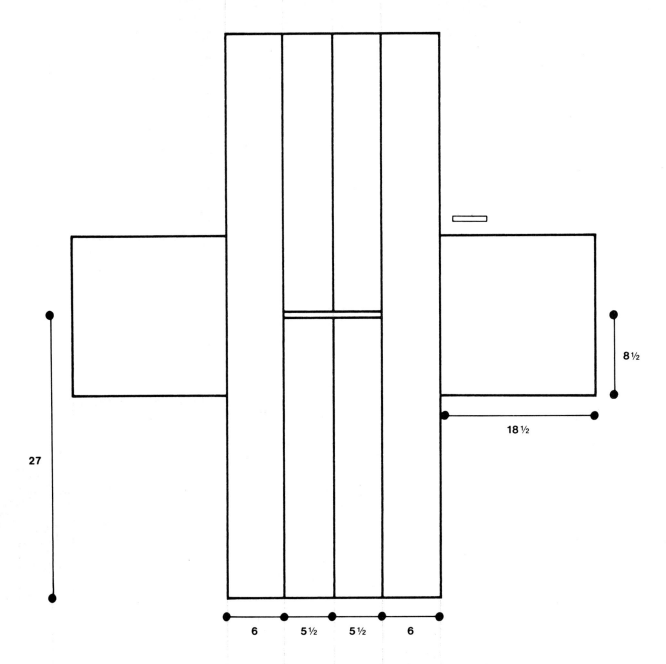

8½

18½

27

6   5½   5½   6

Plotting geometric patterns is another way
to vary the fabric for the modular pullover.

Materials: Super Heavy Donegal Tweed (4 oz skns): (A) 9 mixed naturals, (B) 2
dark brown, (C) 1 natural. Total Yardage: A—1125, B—250, C—125. Hook: Size
J. Gauge: 3 scr = 1″. Stitch: Scr. Size: 6′, 38-32-36. It is easy to plot a pattern
once you know the number of stitches in a row and the number of rows in each
rectangle. To find this out, make a small swatch in the chosen yarn and count the
number of stitches and rows per inch, then multiply. For instance, if the swatch
has 3 stitches to the inch and 2 rows to the inch, a 28″ by 7″ rectangle will have 28
times 3, or 84 stitches in the row, and have 7 times 2 or 14 rows. To plot a design,
make a drawing or use graph paper, letting the squares represent the stitches and
rows. Or make the design up as you work along, crocheting in squares, triangles,
figures, objects, or other forms.

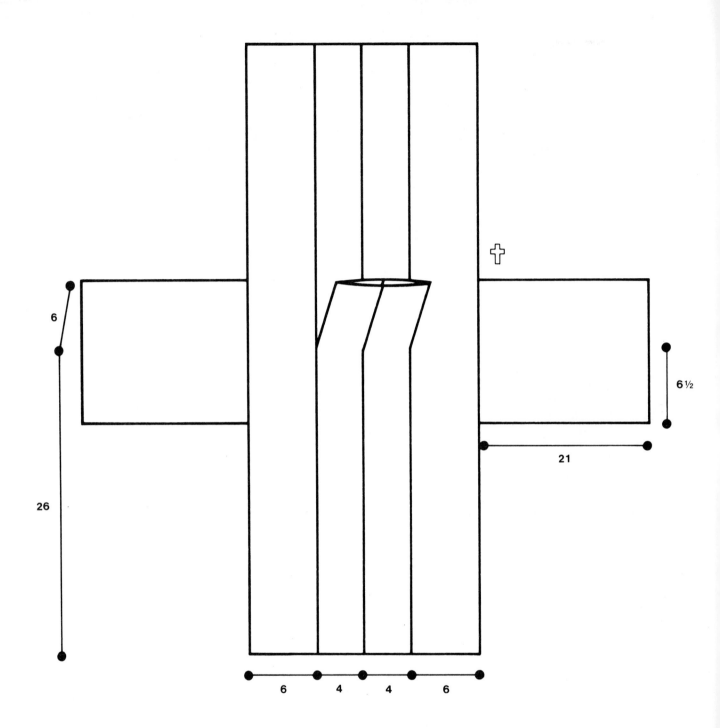

6

26

6½

21

✠

6   4   4   6

To make a garment that will look good and wear well
choose a high quality yarn and work the pullover into a classic shape.

Materials: Naturelle (3.5 oz skns): 12 flecked natural. Total Yardage: 960. Hook: Size J. Gauge: 5 hdcr = 2″. Stitch: Hdcr. Size: 6′, 38-32-36. High quality yarns cost more for good reasons. The section on yarns explains how fibers are graded. Better yarns have a finer luster and are stronger; they age beautifully and soften and mellow with time. We have selected a yarn spun from the wool of the Merino sheep. Bred in the times of Julius Caesar, this sheep produces fleece that is one of the finest, softest, and strongest available.

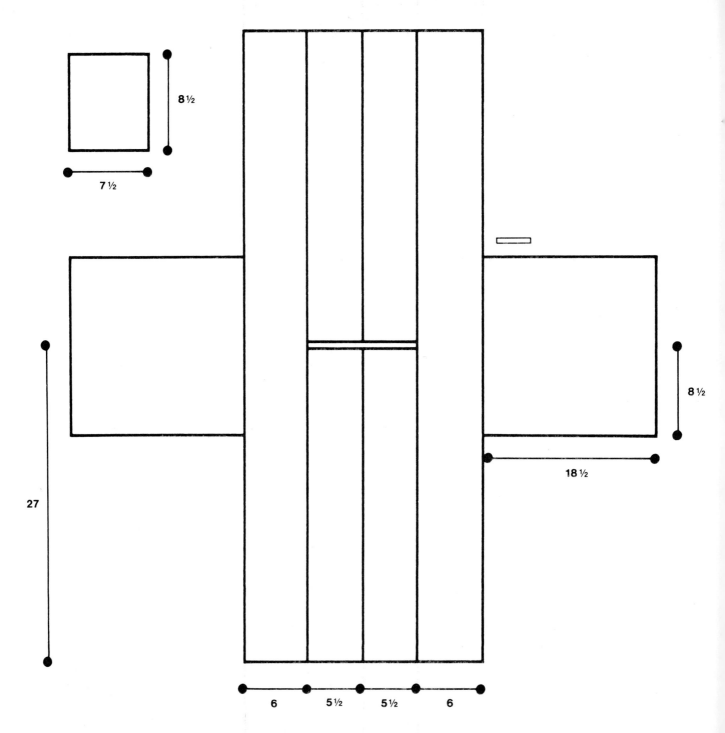

Choose a soft cotton chenille
to make a comfortable boat-neck pullover for informal wear.

Materials: 6 cut Cotton Chenille (4 oz skns): 11 beige. Total Yardage: 1232. Hook: Size J. Gauge: 5 scr = 1″. Stitch: Scr. Size: 6′, 38-32-36. Chenille is made by twisting short cut fibers into a central continuous strand. This makes a tufted yarn, or pile, that is soft and fluffy; and the resulting fabric is loose and supple, so it feels good against the skin. The two patch pockets are rectangles whipstitched into place.

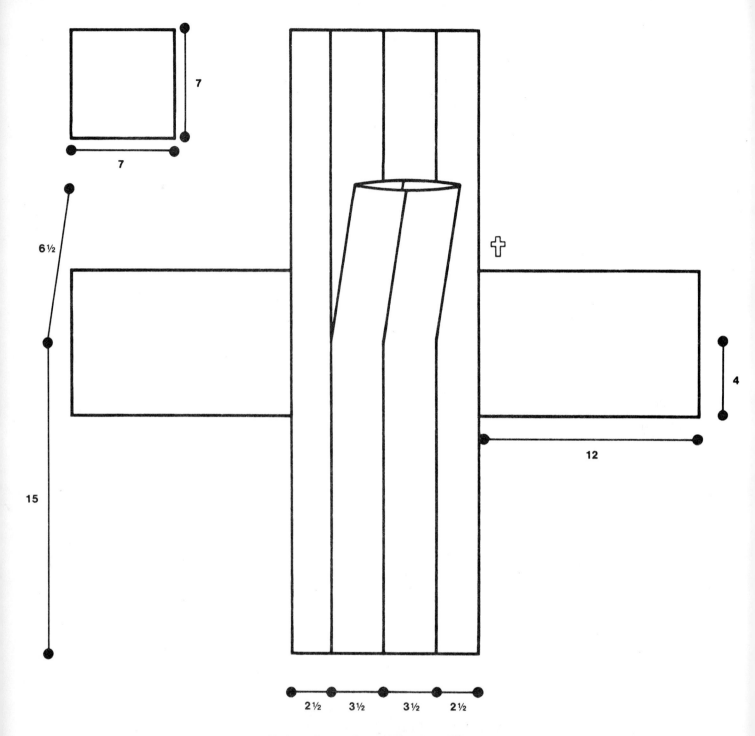

Work each set of rectangles in a different stitch.

Materials: Blarneyspun (2 oz skns): 5 barley. Total Yardage: 520. Hook: Size J. Gauge: 3 scr = 1″. Stitches: Scr, hdcr. Size: 49″, 21, 20, 25. Working the rectangles in different stitches allows for many variations; here is one that is easy to do. Rectangles 1 through 4: Work in the scr. Rectangles 5 and 6: Work in the hdcr. Rectangles 7 and 8 (sleeves): Work in the hdcr to within a few inches of the wrist; work cuff in the scr. Pocket: Work in the scr and from the center out just as with rectangles 1 and 2. Whipstitch into place.

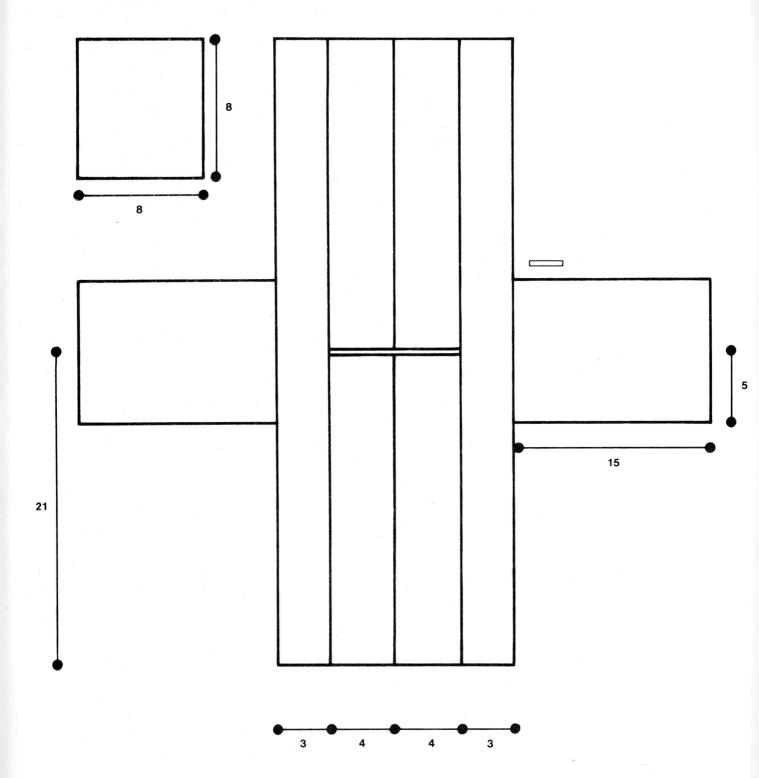

To make ribbing of different widths, alternate rows of stitches in different lengths.

Materials: Blarneyspun (2 oz skns): 9 oatmeal. Total Yardage: 936. Hook: Size J. Gauge: 3 scr = 1″. Stitches: Scr, hdcr. Size: 57″, 27, 31, 26. Rectangles 1 through 4: Work row 1 in the scr, then alternate 2 rows hdcr, 2 rows scr throughout. Pocket: Make a chain to desired length, then work from the center out in the same stitches and width as with rectangles 1 and 2.

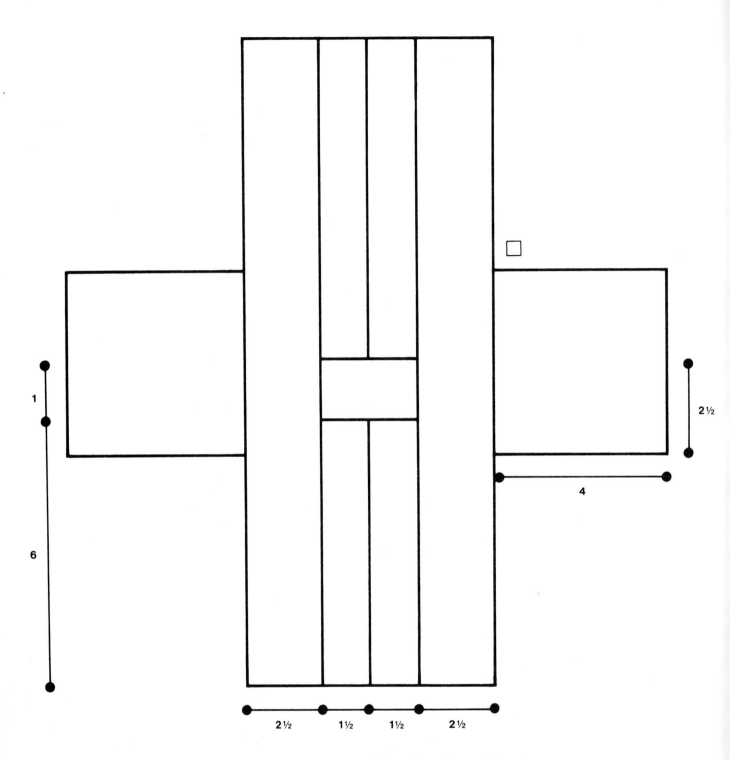

For a newborn baby crochet the modular pullover in a soft fingering yarn

Materials: Gleneagle Fingering Yarn (1 oz skns): 2 white. Total Yardage: 420. Hook: Size 0. Gauge: 9 dcr = 1″. Stitch: Dcr. Size: 4 months. Baby sweaters require yarns that do not shed and that are soft and flexible. When crocheting, do not work the yarn too tightly or you will end up with a stiff fabric that restricts movement. To make a comfortable nightgown, crochet the pullover extra long and, if desired, work in multicolored stripes or fancy stitch patterns.

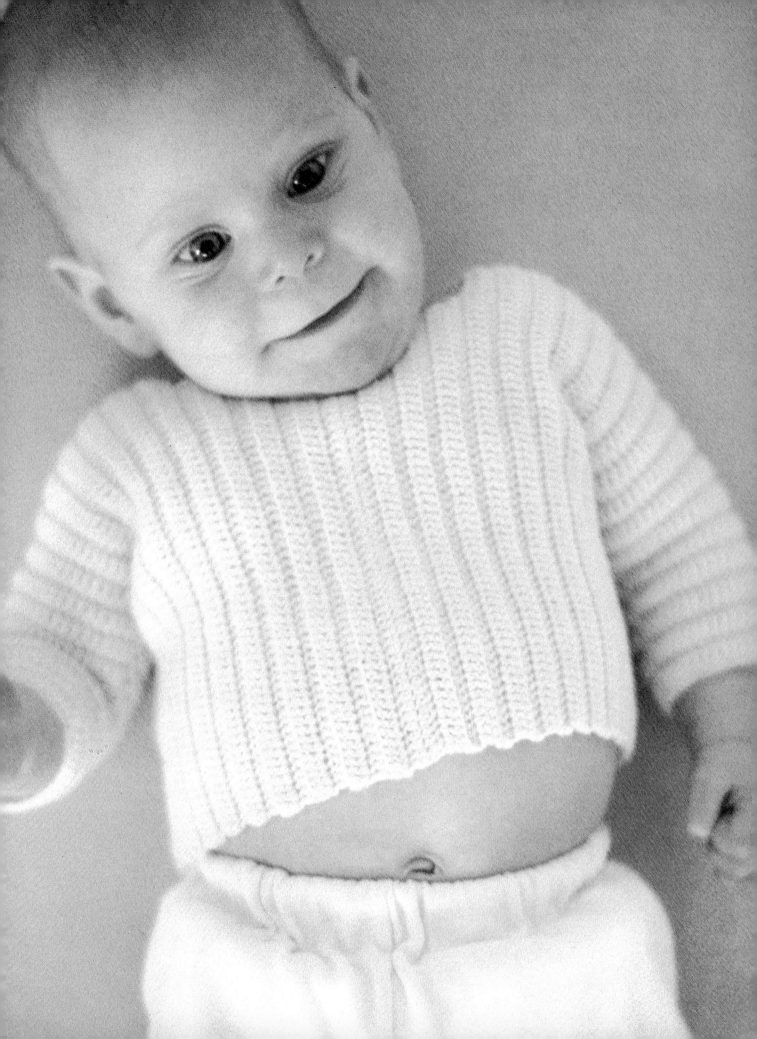

Lesson 5
How to Work on Your Own

To work on your own in the modular way you will be following the procedures you learned in *Lessons 1* through *4*. To sum up, you will be:

1. Joining six or eight rectangles as shown and described in *Lesson 1.*
2. Varying neck styles as described in the step-by-step diagrams.
3. Working with the diagrams for guidance in sizing and styling.
4. Using the various themes in the color photographs as points of departure.

When starting out it is best to make easy things. Experiment with plain yarns and the simpler styles until you are comfortable with the fundamentals of fitting, can maintain tension to keep the right size, and know the way a fabric behaves and drapes when worked in different yarns and widths. A primary virtue of making garments from rectangles is that you quickly learn how different effects are achieved. Then you will be ready to try the more dramatic silhouettes and neck styles worked in fabrics of mixed yarns, colors, and stitches, or in different stripe patterns or textured yarns. In teaching Modular Crochet, it has been our experience that crocheters who have never worked on their own before are usually a little nervous—the idea is so new to them—and they may make some mistakes at first. But for the most part these errors are minor ones and to be expected. Anyone who has developed any skill, whether it be playing tennis or baking bread, knows and accepts the fact that mistakes are part of the learning process. As crocheters learn the modular method, their enthusiasm and confidence grow; after only two or three garments their skills are such that they have the freedom to select any yarn they wish and work it up into a garment to fit any size person in any style. No longer are they limited to the styling and sizes offered by traditional written instructions. To serve as guidelines, the following section has photographs of silhouettes and suggestions of things to consider when you embark on projects of your own.

Function

When considering styles and yarns, think about how the garment will be worn and let its function influence the direction you take. Delicate yarns, for example, are not suitable for a hiking sweater; while wide-sleeved pullovers are lovely, they are not always practical; or, fringes have their charm but sometimes get in the way.

Silhouette

Tight or loose, short or long, necklines, pockets, and cuffs—silhouette changes are the easiest way to modify the modular pullover. As you become more experienced try some of the more dramatic shapes, such as wide ponchos, long hoods, the bloused or the smocked silhouettes. Use the photographs and diagrams for design ideas and guidance in sizing. Note how a silhouette changes when a garment is 12, 20, or 30 inches wide.

Yarn

A classic solution, and one of the most satisfying, is to choose a single yarn and let the beauty of the fiber speak for itself. Or, combine different yarns; they can be mixed in any way that pleases you. Choose the right type and thickness for the style and length. Bloused garments, for example, usually work best in soft, loosespun yarns. When making a long garment make sure the yarn you have chosen will not make the finished piece too heavy. To avoid errors of this kind figure out the final weight of your project before you start to work. For full discussion on yarns and yardages, consult the section *About Yarn*.

Color

Low-key colors of the same intensity make subtle, diffuse patterns. Colors that go from dark to light make rhythmic, undulating patterns. Contrasting colors make strong, bold, vibrant patterns. While there are basic color theories and formulas, for the most part people learn about color by working on their own through observation and experimentation. And, depending on your intuition and what you are trying to accomplish, you will evolve your own ways of combining colors. Some crocheters enjoy the challenge of working with many colors; others prefer single or neutral colors so the form will predominate. Working in a single color offers few problems. Choose one that looks good on you and that suits the style you have selected. If you want to use more than one color, the possibilities are endless. Consider making each row or each set of rectangles in a different color. Or use yarns that are multicolored, such as tweeds, variegated yarns, or heather yarns in dyed or natural colors. All make richly hued fabrics. Or work around themes; earth tones, rainbow colors, reds and pinks.

Stitch

The ridge stitch can be worked in a number of ways. Consider fabrics of random or repeat patterns, or make each rectangle or part of a rectangle in a different stitch. The section *About Stitches and Detailing* discusses the three stitches used.

Hook

Make swatches in various hook sizes until you get the effect you want.

Swatches

Swatches are the best way to experiment with yarns, colors, and stitches, to see how they look and behave when combined in different ways. Keep swatches for future reference, assembling your own collection; later on you will probably find ways to use them. Nothing goes to waste when you make long rectangular swatches; they can always be used for scarves, handbags, and head wraps.

Detailing

Refer to the section *About Stitches and Detailing.*

Fitting

Long garments made of relatively large pieces of fabric stretch a bit when completed and hanging on the body. To compensate for this, work row 1 a little shorter than desired length. The following measurements work in most cases, but ultimately it depends on the type of yarns used and the tension at which they are worked. Work 1 inch shorter for garments at the knee. Work 2 inches shorter for garments at midcalf. Work 3 inches shorter for garments to the ankle. To acquaint yourself with all the variables, make shorter garments first and note how the different yarns behave when worked in your hand. In making allowances for stretching it is best to err on the short side, since garments can always be blocked if they need to be longer. Blocking can shorten a garment too, but this makes the garment wider, since the fabric has to go somewhere when the dimensions are changed. *Lessons 1* and *2* have more information on other aspects of fitting.

Although these elements have been discussed individually in a certain order, the creative process means thinking about all of them simultaneously, then bringing together the separate elements in a harmonious way. How you do it, of course, is what will give your particular modular pullover its special distinction, making it like no other. To plan a design, you can visualize it in your mind or make up drawings or you can select yarns and colors that you find inspiring and let your ideas grow and evolve as the project progresses. Experiment to find the method that best suits your temperament.

Garments made from rectangles
can take many forms
depending on the size
of the rectangles.
Note how a few inches
completely alters a silhouette.
The different widths in order are
14 inches, 18 inches, 23 inches, 30 inches.

As the body of the garment
is made larger,
the sleeves usually
widen in proportion.
The right combination of widths
makes the parts
a harmonious whole.
The different sleeve widths
in order are
5½ inches, 6 inches, 8 inches, 12 inches.

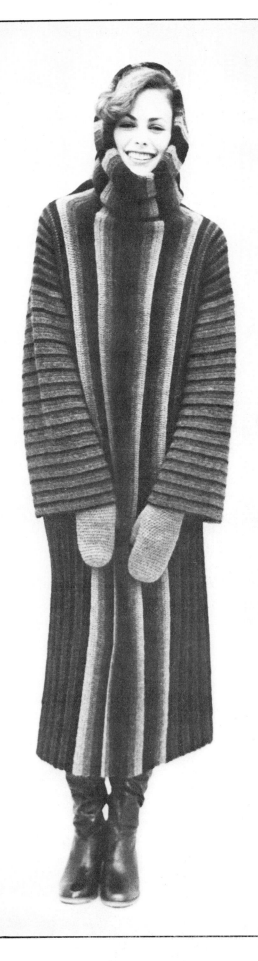

Crochet pullovers
can be worn
straight and loose
or pulled up and bloused.
The bigger the blouse,
the shorter the length.
If the neck
is also a long tube,
even more variations
are possible.

About Stitches and Detailing

Many things go into making a fine garment: high quality fibers, the right choice of yarns, stitches, and colors for function and style, the right proportions for the body type in order to make it a good fit, and finally, good detailing. In developing the modular method, care was taken to make fine detailing not only an inherent part of the process but quick and easy to do. Crocheting garments vertically makes especially beautiful seams because the edges of the fabric are formed by the tops of the stitches. The stitches are easy to see and sew up neatly. Making the sleeves a continuation of the body of a garment, rather than attaching them later with a sewn seam, avoids extra bulk around the armhole and makes the lines of the drop shoulder more pleasing to the eye. Working sleeves in the round automatically makes a fine-looking seam, and, once you have learned how, it is easier and faster than a sewn seam. Joining with a loop is an easy and direct procedure. The loop formed is the same as the loops on the tops of the other stitches, so it is undetectable, and there are no extra threads to make unsightly bulges. When developing your own working techniques, the main thing is to find the most direct and simple method or solution and then to be systematic and consistent in following it through. Sew in end threads in the same way—that is, straight up the row. For seams, join corresponding stitches in order and work under the same threads in every single stitch. Tension is important, and this, again, involves being consistent. A crochet stitch is a series of loops: try to make them all the same size. For example, the last loop of a stitch determines how far apart the stitches will be; if it is a different size each time, the stitches will not be evenly spaced. To get a neat edge, make the loops in the turning chain the same size and always turn corners in the same way—clockwise. Good, efficient working habits keep simple projects simple, produce professional results, and make the entire creative experience relaxing and enjoyable.

About Tools and Materials

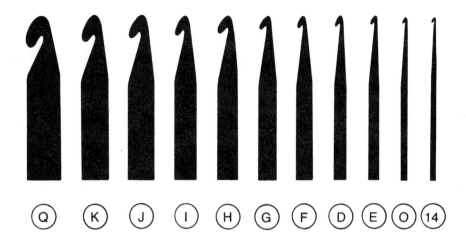

Hooks are made in steel, aluminum, plastic, and wood and come in a wide range of sizes. The smallest are the steel hooks starting at size 14; the largest are the extra big plastic hooks, Q, R, and S. Each size is meant to be used with a certain size thread—the thicker the yarn, the bigger the hook—unless, of course, you are after special effects. Aluminum hooks are the most popular, for they are strong, smooth, and lightweight. They come in the sizes most commonly used: C, the smallest, to K, the largest. It is a good idea to acquire a full range of sizes so you will feel free to work and experiment. When purchasing a hook, select one with a smooth shank and a rounded groove and tip so the yarn will slide on and off easily as you work. Sometimes the yarn catches on wooden hooks. If so, fine sandpaper will smooth the surface. The indentation in the middle of the hook is where you rest the thumb and fingers. The thick part, between the indentation and where the hook thins down, determines the size of the crochet loops and, therefore, the size of the stitch. Some crocheters have a tendency to tighten the tension of the yarn to a different degree each time they draw the loop off the thick part, making the loops differ in size, thereby resulting in uneven stitches. However, if the yarn is kept at the same tension each time the loop is drawn off, the thick part of the hook will perform its function and make even stitches. The hook sizes given in the instructions are for the average hand—that is, for those who work at a medium tension. If you do not get the right gauge, change the tension of the yarn or switch to a different size hook. When working on your own, consult the diagrams. They give the average hook size for different type yarns. Also, the section *About Yarns* has additional information.

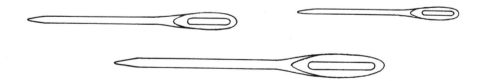

Yarn needles, often called tapestry needles, come in different sizes for different thicknesses of yarn and have rounded, blunt ends so they will draw easily through the loops without splitting or catching the yarns. They have extra large eyes, which make them easier to thread. Use them for sewing in end threads and whipstitching seams. The only other necessary tools are scissors and a tape measure.

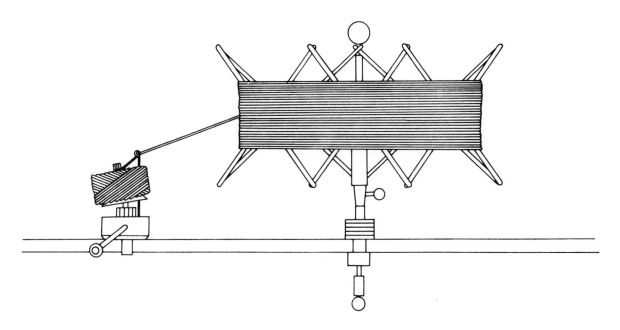

Yarn winders and swifts will save you time. Many of the more unusual yarns come from small specialized yarn mills that do not have the expensive equipment necessary to put yarn up on balls or pull skeins. This means you have to wind the yarn yourself. If you do a lot of crocheting you may want to invest in a yarn winder and swift. The swift is clamped to a table and unfolds to hold the skein of yarn. The yarn is then attached to the spindle of the yarn winder, and the handle is turned to make a neat compact pull skein or ball. Many yarn stores have this equipment for customer use. By all means learn to use it; you will save yourself a lot of time.

Yarn for crocheting usually comes in three different forms: a pull skein, a cone, or a loosely twisted skein. For the pull skein or cone all you have to do is find the loose end, and you are ready to begin work. If you do not have access to a yarn winder and swift, the twisted skein has to be wound by hand. To do this, untwist the yarn, being careful not to tangle the strands, and arrange it around the back of a chair or someone's outstretched arms, or sit down and loop it around your knees. Stretch the yarn tightly so it won't tangle as it is taken from the skein. Smooth the yarn, then untie the threads—there are usually two or three—that keep the yarn in place. Find the end that winds most easily from the skein, and wind the yarn loosely into a ball. If you have found the right end and have not tangled the yarn, it should come off in an orderly fashion. Remember, it was put on in that way. It is very important to wind the yarn loosely. Winding the yarn tightly may cause it to lose some elasticity because it stretches out and puts a strain on the twisted plies. To straighten the kinks out of the yarn that has been worked, loop the yarn into a skein form, tie it in three or four places, immerse it in water, and then gently squeeze out the excess moisture. After rolling it in a towel, dry it, pulling just tightly enough to smooth out the kinks.

About Tension and Gauge

Tension is the amount of pressure applied to the yarn as it is being worked. Tension is controlled by how tightly or loosely the yarn is held as it is run through the fingers and wrapped around the hook. The combination of the tension at which the yarn is worked and the size of the hook will determine the size of the loops and, therefore, the size of the stitches. Yarn worked tightly or a hook that is too small for the thickness of the yarn will produce small loops, making tight stitches and a compact fabric. Yarn worked at what is called a medium or average tension on the right size hook for the thickness of the yarn will make medium sized loops and a stitch and fabric that is firm but still soft and flexible. Yarn worked loosely or a hook that is too large for the thickness of the yarn will produce large loops making a loose stitch and fabric. Each of these different size stitches will result in a different gauge. Gauge is the number of stitches to the inch. The idea is to strive for a medium tension in order to get the best gauge for the thickness of the yarn, thereby producing a firm but soft fabric. If the stitches are worked too tightly, the fabric will lose its suppleness and elasticity and become stiff and uncomfortable. If the stitches are worked too loosely, the fabric will be weak and flimsy, and it may stretch or sit out. Sometimes, of course, the tension is purposely distorted for special effects. Once you start working, maintain the same tension throughout the piece. Some crocheters have a tendency to change the tension as they work along. If the tension is tightened after the work is started, the garment will get shorter; if the tension is loosened, the garment will grow longer. But if the tension is maintained, the piece should keep its shape and size. Some crocheters find that their work changes no matter how carefully they try to maintain the tension. Therefore, they purposely make the first row a little longer or shorter knowing from experience that the fabric will eventually shrink or stretch a bit. It is better if the garment is too short rather than too long, since it can always be blocked to the desired size. When working on your own, make up a small swatch to see if the hook size you have chosen makes a firm but soft fabric. If you are not happy with the results, you can switch hooks or change the tension of the yarn as you work it. To get a looser, more supple fabric, loosen up on the tension of the yarn or switch to a larger hook. To get a tighter, firmer fabric, tighten up on the tension of the yarn or switch to a smaller hook. With a little experience you will soon have a good idea of what hook size works best for your hand in the different weight yarns to get the ideal firm but soft fabric.

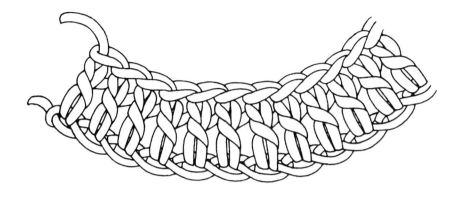

Make the chain and the stitches with the same amount of tension. If the stitches are worked in a tighter tension than the chain, the work curls up. To correct this you either have to loosen the tension of the stitches or tighten the tension of the chain.

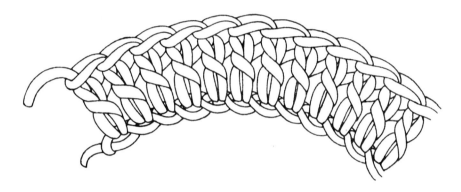

If the stitches are worked in a looser tension than the chain, the work fans out. To correct this you either have to tighten the tension of the stitches or loosen the tension of the chain.

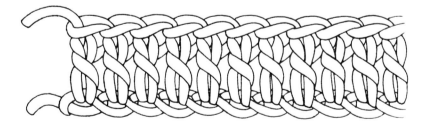

When the chain and stitches are worked in the same tension, and the same tension is maintained throughout, the crocheted piece will lie flat, straight, and even.

About the Stitches

All the garments in this book are designed to be crocheted using one or more of three basic stitches:
1. The single crochet ridge stitch.
2. The half double crochet ridge stitch.
3. The double crochet ridge stitch.

The single crochet ridge, half double crochet ridge, and double crochet ridge stitches are the same as the regular single, half double, and double crochet stitches, except that you insert the hook in only the back loop of each stitch when working the rows, causing a ridge to be formed. Many of the styles in *Modular Crochet* can be made using other stitches, and you may want to experiment with others once you are familiar with how the modular shape behaves. For our purposes we have chosen to limit ourselves to the ridge stitch because, when comparing crocheted fabrics, you will find that the one made using the ridge stitch is the most flexible and has the most elasticity. A crocheted garment made from rectangles can be thought of as a box; and if the fabric is not structured properly or is not supple enough, it will continue to look like a box after it is put on. It will also have a tendency to bunch up under the arms, making the garment uncomfortable. However, when a fabric has elasticity, as the ridge stitch fabric does, it is supple; it stretches to fit around the body and lies smoothly on the curves, giving the garment pleasing contours and a good fit. To make the lines even softer and more flattering and to provide for a slimming effect, the rows are worked vertically, creating a sleek silhouette with long, graceful, flowing lines, whether the fabric clings to the body or is wide enough to fall into folds. Take special note that for the ridge stitch, you do not work into the turning chain at the end of the row, and you do work into the first stitch at the beginning of a row. The natural edge that is formed has a beautiful scallop and usually does not require any trim or edging. And, finally, note that each stitch makes a fabric of a different type, texture, and ridge (in width and depth); for every thickness of yarn each stitch makes a fabric of a different thickness. Using the same yarn, it gets thicker in this order: dcr, hdcr, scr.

Abbreviations

ch	chain
sc	single crochet
scr	single crochet ridge
hdc	half double crochet
hdcr	half double crochet ridge
dc	double crochet
dcr	double crochet ridge
skn(s)	skein(s)
oz(s)	ounce(s)

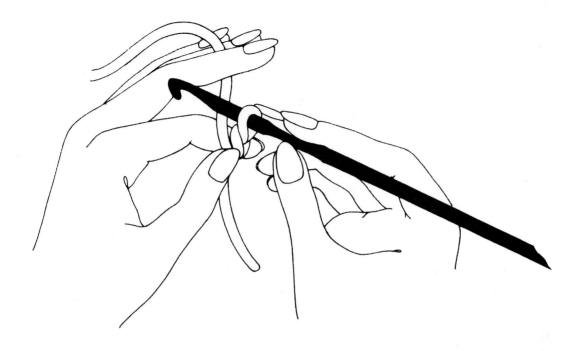

How to Hold the Yarn and Hook

With the thicker yarns used today it is not necessary to run
the yarn through all the fingers in the traditional way.
Try this simpler method. The thumb and forefinger
of the left hand hold and stabilize the worked yarn.
The unworked yarn is held between the middle
and ring fingers. These fingers control the tension.
These two fingers also place the yarn on the hook.
The right hand holds the hook like a pencil,
with the thumb and forefinger fitting into the indentation.

How to Start

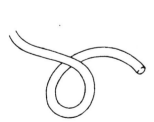  

1. Form a loop
with the end of the yarn.

2. Insert the hook into the loop
and pull the yarn
from the ball through the loop.

3. Holding the loose yarn end,
pull the yarn from the ball
to tighten the loop on the hook.

How to Work
the Chain Stitch

1. Yarn over the hook.
Pull the yarn through
the loop on the hook.

2. One chain stitch made.

3. Repeat steps 1 and 2
to make a series of chain stitches
until the chain is the desired length.

How to Make
the Single Crochet
Ridge Stitch
(scr)

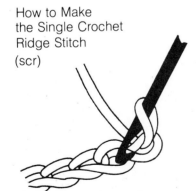

1. Make a chain to desired length.
Insert hook under the 2 top threads
of 2nd chain stitch from hook.
Do not count loop on hook.

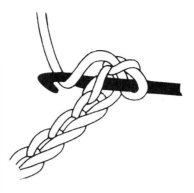

2. Yarn over hook.

3. Draw up a loop.

4. Yarn over hook.

5. Draw through 2 loops on hook.
One single crochet stitch made.

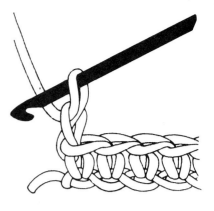

6. Make one single crochet
in each chain across.
At end of row, chain 1, turn.
Always turn the work in the same way.
Flip the crocheted piece over,
from right to left,
like the page of a book.

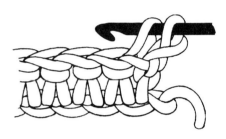

7. Next Rows
Working under only the back loop
of each stitch
(the loop further from you)
to form a ridge (scr),
make one single crochet in first stitch
(2nd loop *from* hook),
and in each stitch across.

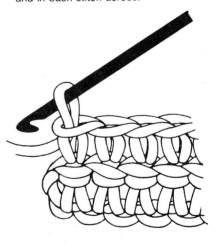

8. At end of row, make the last stitch
in top of last single crochet
of previous row.
Do not work into the turning chain.
Chain 1, turn.

174

How to Make
the Half Double Crochet
Ridge Stitch (hdcr)

1. Make a chain
to desired length.

2. Yarn over hook.

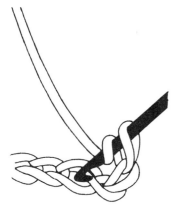

3. Insert hook under
the 2 top threads
of 3rd chain stitch from hook.
Do not count loop on hook.

4. Draw up a loop.

5. Yarn over hook.

6. Draw yarn through
all 3 loops on hook.
One half double crochet
stitch made.

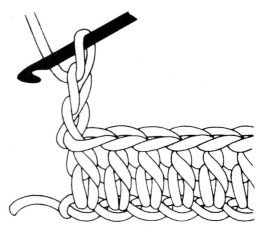

7. Make one half double crochet in each chain
across. At end of row, chain 2, turn.
Always turn the work in the same way.
Flip the crocheted piece over,
from right to left, like the page of a book.

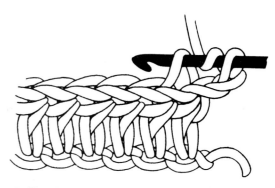

8. Next Rows
Working under only the back loop of each stitch
(the loop further from you) to form a ridge
make one half double crochet in first stitch
(3rd loop *from* hook), and in each stitch across.

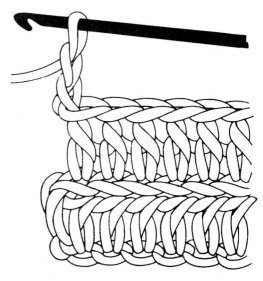

9. At end of row, make the last stitch
in top of last half double crochet of previous row.
Do not work into the turning chain. Chain 2, turn.

How to Make
the Double Crochet
Ridge Stitch
(dcr)

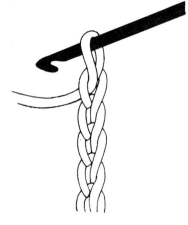

1. Make a chain to desired length.

2. Yarn over hook.

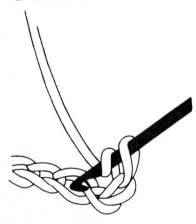

3. Insert hook under
the 2 top threads
of 3rd chain stitch from hook.
Do not count loop on hook.

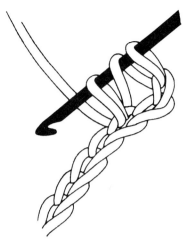

4. Draw up a loop.

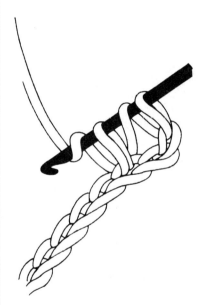

5. Yarn over hook.

6. Draw through 2 loops.

7. Yarn over hook.

8. Draw through 2 loops.
One double crochet stitch made.

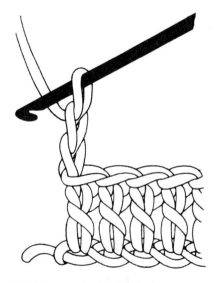

9. Make one double crochet
in each chain across.
At end of row, chain 2, turn.
Always turn the work in the same way.
Flip the crocheted piece over,
from right to left,
like the page of a book.

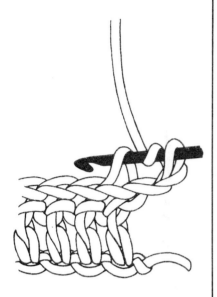

10. Next Rows
Working under only
the back loop of each stitch
(the loop further from you)
to form a ridge (dcr),
make one double crochet
in first stitch
(3rd loop *from* hook),
and in each stitch across.

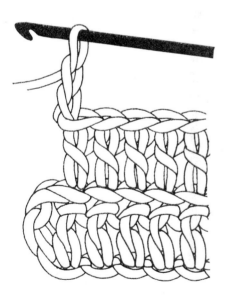

11. At end of row,
make the last stitch
in top of last double crochet
of previous row.
Do not work into the turning chain.
Chain 2, turn.

How to Read Stitches

Crocheting is less confusing if you take a few minutes to familiarize yourself with the characteristics of the different stitches and learn how to read them. The following will help you. Each stitch and row has a front and a back—a right and a wrong side—and each side has special features that help you to identify it. With most stitches, the front side of the stitches are smoother, and the backs are more elaborate and bumpy. Look at a large piece of fabric and note how the rows alternate between smooth, bumpy, smooth; these are the right, wrong, right side of the stitches. If this guideline does not help you, then single out a special feature that you easily recognize and that is common to each stitch made in a row, and use it to identify the stitches and rows. When following instructions that say "wrong side of stitch facing you," look to see if the bumpy side of the stitch is facing you. Compare the stitch to the illustrations shown here to see if it matches. To count stitches, think of each stitch as a vertical tube and single out each tube as you move across the row, or note that each stitch has an eyelet or loop on the top. Count the loops across the row. The illustrations have numbered stitches that help you to identify a single stitch.

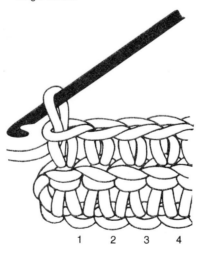

1   2   3   4

1. The bottom row shows the back or wrong side of the scr stitch. The top row shows the front or right side of the scr stitch. The numbers identify the single stitches.

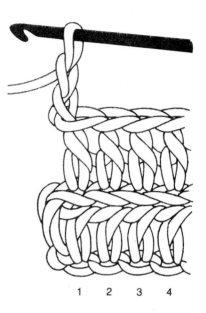

1   2   3   4

2. The bottom row shows the back or wrong side of the hdcr stitch. The top row shows the front or right side of the hdcr stitch. The numbers identify the single stitches.

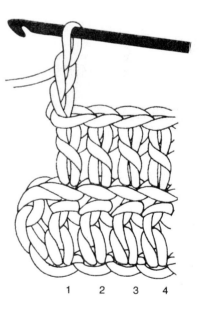

1   2   3   4

3. The bottom row shows the back or wrong side of the dcr stitch. The top row shows the front or right side of the dcr stitch. The numbers identify the single stitches.

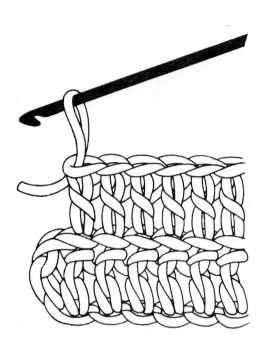

How to End Off

1. When the last stitch in the row is complete, cut the yarn, leaving an end thread of 4 inches or so. Do not cut the yarn too short or the stitch may come apart; also, a longer thread is easier to sew in or work over.

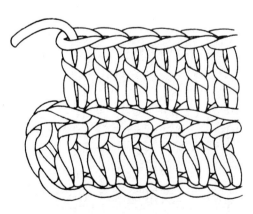

2. Pull the loop on the hook up, and then out. This is sufficient to lock the stitch in place.

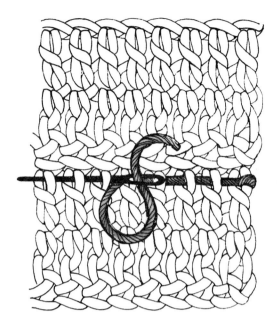

How to Sew in End Threads

In most cases you can crochet over the end threads as you work along, but sometimes they have to be sewn in. To do this, thread a yarn needle with the end thread and, working on the wrong side of the fabric and straight up the row, draw the yarn through the bottom loops of a few stitches, make a back stitch to secure the yarn, then draw the yarn through a few more stitches. Be careful not to split the yarns. Do not work back and forth across the rows. Sewing all the end threads in one spot causes bulges, and the fabric won't hang straight and even. Avoid this, especially, at the underarm.

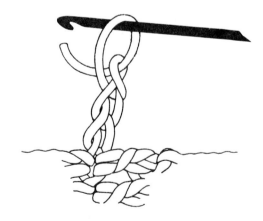

How to Remove Extra Loops in the Chain

*Insert hook into the end loop of the chain and pull the loop out. Repeat from * until all of the extra loops are removed.

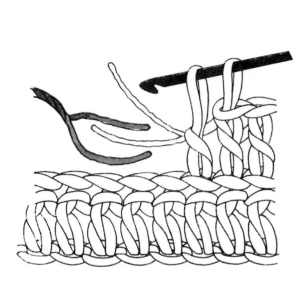

How to Splice Yarn

1. With plied yarns you can attach new yarns within the row by splicing them, thereby avoiding a knot within the fabric. Work the last stitch in the old yarn to the last 2 loops on the hook. Cut the yarn leaving an end thread of about 6 inches. Split the plies into 2 equal parts. Split 6 inches of the new yarn in the same way.

3. Finish the stitch with the newly twisted yarn and work the next 2 or 3 stitches. Carefully snip off the 4 end threads. If all this is neatly done you will not be able to tell where the old yarn leaves off and the new begins. Splicing yarns may seem awkward at first, but with a little practice it is easy to do.

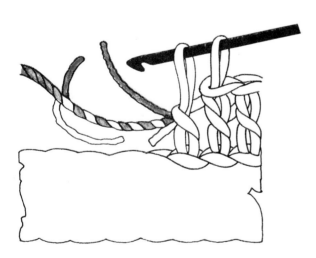

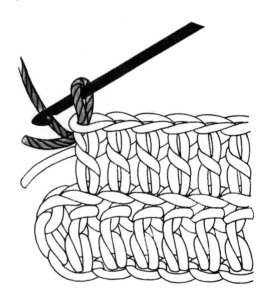

2. Twist half of the new split yarn around half of the old split yarn to make 6 inches of newly twisted yarn in the original thickness. For extra assurance twist the leftover, long end threads once or twice around the newly twisted yarn.

How to Attach New Yarn

Whenever possible, attach new yarn at the end of a row to avoid a knot within the fabric. Exceptions would be when you add a new color or a different yarn within the row. To do either, work in the following way. Work the last stitch to the last 2 loops on the hook. Drop the old yarn and complete the stitch in the new yarn. Cut the old yarn, leaving an end thread of 4 inches or so. Lay the end thread on top of the next stitches and work over it or sew it in later on.

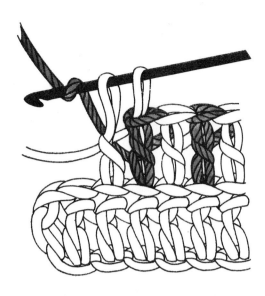

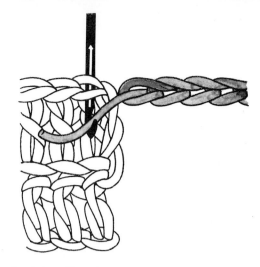

How to Make Stitches in Different Colors or Yarns

Stitches in alternate colors: A is first color, B is second color. *Work A to last 2 loops on hook. Drop A to the *right*. Complete stitch with B. Work B to last 2 loops on hook. Drop B to the *left*. Pick up A and complete the stitch. Repeat from *. Always drop A to the right and B to the left so the yarns won't get twisted. Working more than one stitch in a color: Lay the yarn that you are not using on top of the stitches and crochet over it until you are ready to use it again. For distances of over 6 inches you may have to cut the yarn and then reattach it to avoid extra bulk.

How to Join with a Loop

1. Joining the neck chain to the crocheted piece, *insert the hook under the 2 top threads of the first stitch, and draw the yarn through.

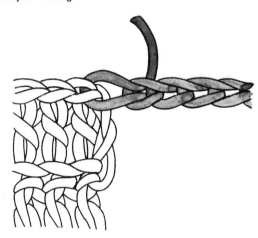

2. Then draw the yarn back into the same opening it came from. Note that this loop looks like and is the same as the loops in the chain and the loops on top of the stitches.

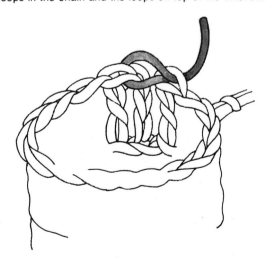

How to Carry Yarn for Alternate Stripes

A is first color, B is second color. *Work 2 rows of A to last stitch in row. Drop A. Make last loop of stitch in B. Work 2 rows of B to last stitch in row. Drop B. Pick up A and make last loop of stitch with A. Repeat from *. *The last loop of the last stitch in the row is made with the alternate color*. To get a neat, uniform edge, always pick up the yarn in the same way and do not pull it too loose or too tight.

3. Joining with a loop in the round for sleeves and edging, repeat from * same as above.

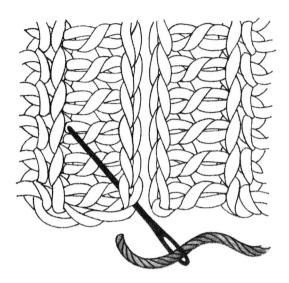

How to Whipstitch Seams

1. Thread a yarn needle with a length of yarn. For a neat seam, work on the right side of the garment so you can see if you are splitting yarns. Place the 2 edges of the crocheted piece together. Starting at the bottom edge, insert the needle from back to front under the 2 top loops of the first stitch on the left. Draw the yarn through leaving a tail of 4 inches.

3. Insert the needle under the 2 top loops of the second stitch on the right and second stitch on the left and draw the yarn through.

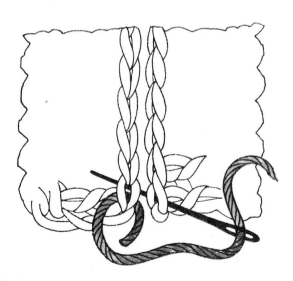

2. Working from the front, insert the needle under the 2 top loops of the first stitch on the right and again under the 2 top loops of the first stitch on the left. Draw the yarn through.

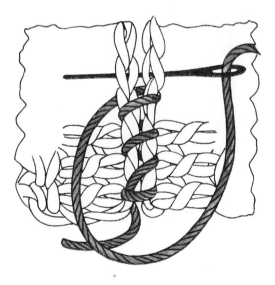

4. Insert the needle under the 2 top loops of the next stitch on each side; draw the yarn through. Repeat from * for the entire seam. Work at a medium tension. If the yarn is drawn too tight, the seam will pucker. If it is too loose, it will draw apart when the garment is put on.

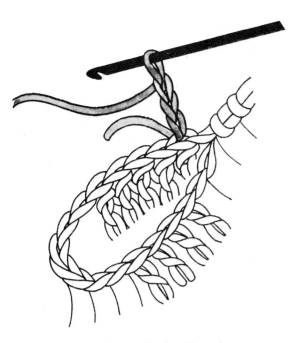

How to Work Sleeves in the Round

Illustrations and directions are for the hdcr and the dcr. Changes for the scr are in parentheses (x).

1. Starting at armhole bottom, with the wrong side of the stitch facing you, draw a loop through only the back loop of the first stitch. Chain 3 (2). Work one ridge stitch in each stitch around.

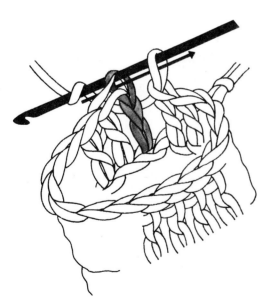

2. When the last stitch of the round is complete, insert the hook into the top loop of the beginning chain 3 (2). Yarn over and draw the yarn through the chain and the loop on the hook. *This is called joining with a slip stitch.*

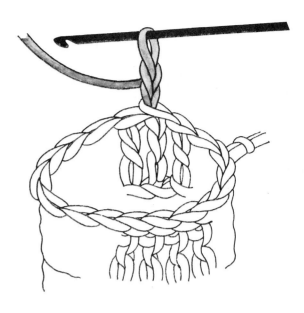

3. Next Round: Chain 2 (1).

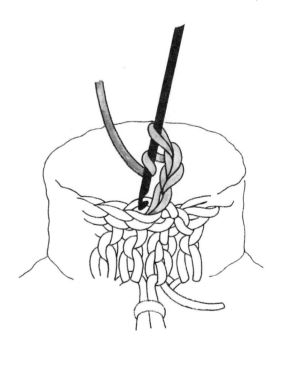

4. Turn the work so the *wrong side of the stitch is facing you.* Work the first stitch under the back thread of the fourth (third) loop from the hook.

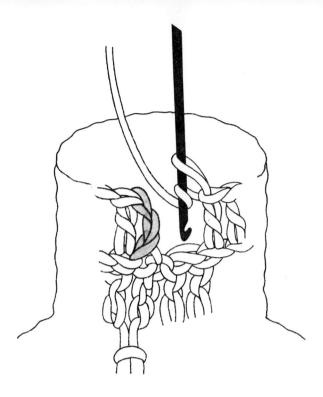

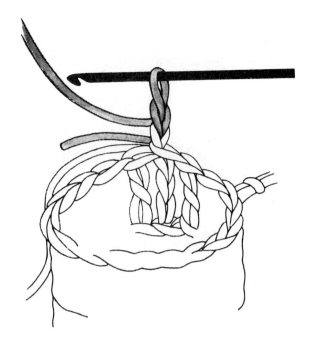

5. Work one ridge stitch in each stitch around, making the last stitch in the top of the last stitch of the previous round. *Do not work into the chain or you will add a stitch.* If you are in doubt, turn the work so you can see the other side and make sure that you have worked into the top of the stitch and not the chain.

How to Carry Yarn and Change Color in the Round

1. When working in stripes, you can carry the yarn from round to round if the distance is not longer than about 1½ inches. With color A, work round 1 and join with a slip stitch. Drop yarn. Make the turning chain in color B.

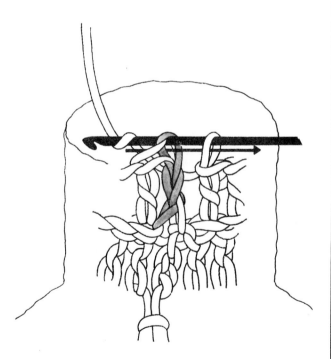

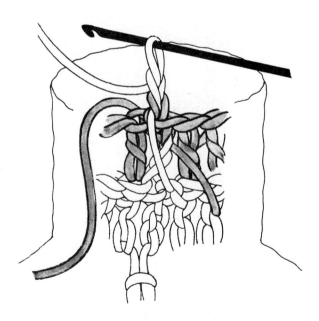

6. Join with a slip stitch into the top of the beginning chain.

Next Rounds: Repeat steps 3-6 until sleeve is desired length, then cut the yarn and join with a loop.

2. Work next round and join with a slip stitch. Drop yarn. Pick up color A and make the turning chain. *The turning chain is always in the next color to be worked.* Do not pull the picked-up yarn too tight or the fabric will pucker. Work the sleeve wrong side out. Always drop yarn and carry yarn on the wrong side of the fabric.

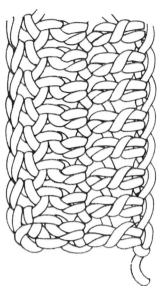

How to Crochet a Sash or Scarf

You work a belt or scarf from the center out just as with the pullovers. Because the beginning chain is in the middle, the piece will hang straighter; also, the edge is neat and uniform because it is the same on both sides.

1. Make a chain the length of the piece. Work in the chosen stitch until the piece is half of the desired width. Cut yarn.

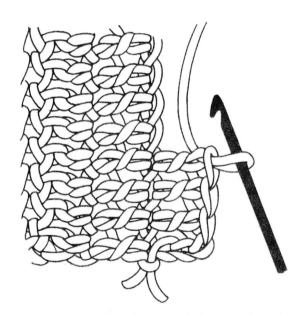

2. Return to row 1. Pull a loop through the bottom loop of the first stitch. Chain 2 for a scr, chain 3 for a hdcr and dcr. Work one stitch in each loop to the end. Work to the same width as the first half. Trim: if you wish, at the end of the last row of each side work 1 row of sc around the end stitches.

How to Crochet a Round Cord

1. Make a chain to desired length.

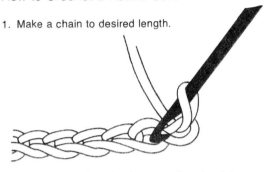

2. Insert the hook under the 2 top threads of the second chain stitch from the hook.

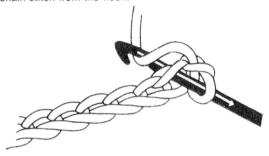

3. Yarn over hook. Draw the yarn through the chain *and* the loop on the hook. One slip stitch made.

4. *Insert the hook under the 2 top threads of the next chain. Yarn over hook. Draw the yarn through the chain *and* the loop on the hook. Repeat from * to the end of the chain. Make sure you work under the 2 top threads and the front of the chain is always facing you. Do not twist the chain. For thicker round cords, work 2 or more strands together in one or more colors. Another variation is to work the chain in one color, then slip stitch back in a second color.

About Yarn

It is an exciting time to be crocheting because today most of us have access to yarns from all over the world, and there is an extraordinary variety, from the richly textured handspun yarns in their natural colors, to the tremendous assortment of synthetics and machinespun yarns which modern technology has made available. Yarns for crocheting can be divided into three categories: natural fibers—wools, cottons, silks, and linens; synthetic fibers—various artificial fibers made from different chemicals; and blends—a combination of natural and synthetic fibers. These various materials, spun into many different thicknesses, are standardized in the following ways: very thin yarns—worked on the steel hooks size 14 through 00; lightweight, or fingering yarns—worked on size C through E hooks; sportweight yarns—worked on F or G hooks; medium weight yarns, or the 4 ply knitting worsteds—worked on G or H hooks; and bulky yarns—worked on I hooks through the big Q and S hooks. The simplest yarns are single, continuous strands—single ply yarns—of any thickness, from a thin cotton to a thick, bulky wool. Plied yarns have 2 or more strands twisted together—2 ply yarns have 2 strands twisted together, 4 ply have 4 strands twisted together. The plies can be all the same thickness, texture, and color, or, as with the novelty yarns, they can be varied in many ways. To give us our wonderful variety of yarns, spinners have devised, over the centuries, many techniques for combining fibers. Yarns have been crimped, looped, coiled, twisted to look like knit tubes, wrapped around central core fibers, space dyed, and polished. All this has been done in order to produce sturdy, utilitarian wools; smooth, sleek rayons; plain cotton strings; shiny, reflective metal threads; tufted chenilles; multicolored tweeds; variegated brushed wools; nubbly bouclés; and furry angoras and mohairs. To see how these different types of yarns look and behave when worked in various ways, consult the color photographs. Observe that each yarn makes a unique fabric with its own special characteristics of texture, feel, and drape. Once crocheters become aware of the many different forms spun fibers can take, they usually want to try them all. With this in mind, the following chart identifies the different type yarns used in this book. Pages 170-1 on tension and gauge explain how to choose the right hook size for different yarn thicknesses when working on your own.

ALPACA: The alpaca animal of South America provides the wool for this yarn. The long, silky hairs in their natural tones make a slightly furry yarn that crochets into a soft, handsome, and informal fabric.

ALPACKA: A heather yarn that is a blend of wool and alpaca. Heather yarns are made by blending several different colors together. Because of the closely related hues, this type yarn is especially pleasing when it is spun from the many natural colors found in an animal's coat.

ANGORA: This exquisite fiber comes from the Belangor Rabbit. Its long hairs make a crocheted fabric that is exceptionally rich and luxurious. There are 2 grades: The lesser grade is from the belly of the rabbit; the better grade is from the back where the hairs are softer and longer, the latter characteristic making the yarn shedproof after a few wearings.

BLARNEYSPUN: A 3 ply Irish wool that is sturdy and long-lasting. In some types, one of the plies has different colors and thicknesses of yarns spun in to make a two-toned, candy stripe yarn. Other types are heather tweeds.

BOUCLE: Each ply is a different thickness twisted at a different tension, causing the fibers to curl and buckle. The resulting yarn is nubbly and kinky. It crochets into a splendid, highly textured fabric.

BRUSHED WOOL: A very long-haired yarn that makes a light, airy, furry fabric. The finished fabric can be left as it is, or it can be brushed to make the hairs even longer. To do this, take a brush with widely spaced teeth—such as one that is used for a dog's coat—and, working in one direction, brush the surface evenly until all the hairs are approximately the same length. You may want to practice on a small swatch first to see how it looks.

CANDIDE LIGHT WEIGHT WOOL: A thick-and-thin yarn spun in heather colors makes a light but compact fabric with a slightly rough texture, so it is perfect for long garments that must be light in weight and informal.

CHENILLE: This yarn is usually made from cotton or rayon blends. When processed it is cut short and twisted into a continuous core yarn. The crocheted fabric has a pile that is soft and fluffy with a velvety appearance; its extra depth makes it feel voluptuous.

CLASSIQUE: A soft sport weight wool imported from France. The way this yarn is spun and twisted makes it look like a knitted tube. The resulting fabric has a fine, sculptural quality because the stitches are well defined and the lights and shadows they cast are sharp and clear.

COLOMBIAN HANDSPUN SHEEPSWOOL: These richly textured yarns are spun thick and thin, which gives the crocheted fabric a rough, uneven texture. It is waterproof because all the natural oils are left in.

COTILLION: An unusual combination of yarns—one of the plies is a soft wool; the other is a shiny metallic synthetic called lurex.

COTTON: This yarn comes in several thicknesses, grades, and types, from the finest Egyptian cottons to the common string found in hardware stores, and each type makes a fabric with its own unique qualities. Cotton lacks elasticity—the ability to stretch then spring back into shape—so be careful when using it for styles where stretch is an important factor. Also it is a relatively heavy yarn. To make sure a garment won't be too heavy, calculate the finished weight before starting a project. Mercerized cotton has been polished to give it a soft luster, or sheen.

DONEGAL TWEEDS: These famous yarns from Ireland are known for their strength, durability, and unusual colors and textures. The yarns are tightly spun to make them crinkle and curl; in the process, nubs of different colors are added in to get the multicolor effect.

GLENEAGLE FINGERING WOOL: Imported from Scotland, this is an extremely soft yarn of the finest quality and crochets into a lovely light weight fabric. Its softness makes it an especially good choice for baby sweaters.

FISHERMAN WOOL: This is a coarse, strong, long-lasting yarn. "Unscoured" means the natural oils are left in to make it waterproof; "scoured" means the yarns have been washed to remove most of the oils.

LOPI AND ICELANDIC HOMESPUN: Imported from Iceland, these yarns come from a long-haired sheep whose fleece can be as long as 19 inches. The loose combing leaves air between the fibers as they are processed, making yarns that are thick but relatively light in weight. Yarns like this are said to have a high loft. When they are crocheted, the fabric is also thick, warm, but light in weight. For a longer nap, or furry look, it can be brushed with a wide-toothed brush.

MELODY: A blend of mohair and acrylic imported from Italy. This is one of the more successful blends. The yarn has a soft luster and feel, instead of the usual harsh sheen and feel that is typical of so many synthetics—especially those that try to simulate the natural fibers.

MERINO WOOL: The sheep producing this fleece were bred in the times of Julius Caesar. It is a fine wool of exceptional quality and makes a soft and durable fabric.

METALLICS: An ornamental yarn made from various synthetic materials. Its unique character is derived from the high gloss of the fibers, making the yarns reflective and the colors brilliant and glowing. "Feu d'Artifice" is special, for it comes in a wide range of unusual colors.

MOHAIR: This long-haired yarn is spun from goats' hair, and the better grades are made from the longer, softer hairs. When long-haired yarns are worked into a fabric they create pockets of air, making the fabric bulky, but soft, airy, and light in weight.

RAYON: An exotic yarn with a smooth, satin finish. Its slipperiness makes it a little more difficult to work with, but once you are used to that characteristic, the yarn works up quickly. The finished fabric is so unusual that it is worth the extra effort. It crochets much more easily if you work more than one strand at a time. To secure the yarn when sewing in end threads, loop it around a strand of yarn and tie it with hitch knots—that is, tie the yarn in on itself two or three times and pull tight. Then snip the end leaving a ¼ inch or so and fluff up the yarn to separate the strands so it won't pull out.

ROMA: A heather-toned, thick-and-thin, light weight wool imported from Sweden. To make a decorative fabric with a subtle, diffuse pattern, work with a multicolored heather yarn such as this.

SCHEEPJES NATUURWOL: A 2 ply heather wool imported from Holland. A blend of many natural colors of sheep's wool, it makes a soft and sturdy fabric.

SHETLAND WOOL: A classic yarn loosely spun from very long, strong fibers. It is made from the fine undercoat of a sheep raised in the Shetland Islands. Crocheted, it makes a handsome, casual fabric with a slight, furry texture.

VARIEGATED WOOL: Any multicolored yarn that is space dyed—which means there are a few inches of each of the colors and the sequence of these colors is repeated throughout the yarn. Depending on the range of colors, a fabric worked in this yarn can be strongly or subtly patterned.

WORSTED: The most common yarn of this type is called knitting worsted. It is a 4 ply yarn and makes a soft, sturdy, medium weight fabric. A popular yarn, it is available in all yarn shops and comes in many grades. The better grades are made from fibers that are longer, softer, and stronger.

About Mixed Yarns

In the technique using mixed yarns, two or more strands of yarn are worked together at the same time. Instructions will read, work X number of strands held together. Even though some crocheters may think so, it is not more difficult to work than a single strand. In fact, mohairs and other long-haired yarns are easier to work because more than one strand makes a more uniform strand, so it slides on and off the hook more easily. To work with mixed yarns there are several ways of preparing the yarn. In the first method the yarns are wound into one large ball before the work is started. To do this, place the separate balls into a container; then, taking a thread from each ball, wind the yarn into a single ball. You may find some yarns have a tendency to kink and curl up. If this is a problem, engage the help of another person; place the balls in that person's lap and let the yarn run through his or her fingers. In this way the yarns are kept taut and are easier to wind. When the ball is wound, work the yarn as you would a single strand of yarn. The second method of preparing mixed yarn is to place the separate balls of yarn into a bag or some other container; then, taking an end from each ball, pull the yarns out together a few feet at a time. Work the yarn up, then pull out another few feet. When a ball runs out, replace it with another ball and continue working as before, crocheting over the end threads. Don't worry about keeping the yarns straight. You need not twist them in any particular way; just keep them fairly smooth and work them as they come from the balls. Occasionally you may find certain yarns will twist of their own accord. When they do, twist them in the opposite direction to straighten them out. If you use a hook with a rounded tip and work at a medium tension, you should not have any problems with the yarns splitting and catching.

About Quantity and Quality When Selecting Yarns

When planning your own designs there are several ways you can determine the amount of yarn you will need for your garment. The simplest solution is to find a good yarn shop with experienced personnel. They will be able to recommend appropriate yarn, hook size, and yarn amounts for the size and style you have in mind. Or, you can use the yardages given for the garments in this book as a guide if the size of the garment, the stitch, and the thickness of the yarn you are using are the same. You can also calculate the yardage yourself by following this simple procedure used by professional designers: Make a 4-inch square swatch in the yarn and stitch you have chosen and keep track of how many yards you have used. Then determine how many 4-inch square swatches there will be in your garment. Next, multiply the number of yards in the swatch by the number of squares in the garment. The resulting figure is the total yardage needed for the garment. Then divide the total yardage by the total yards in the skein. The resulting figure is the total amount of skeins needed for the garment. Here is a shorthand version of the formula: (yards per 4″ square) × (total number of squares) = (total yards for garment); then (total yards for garment) ÷ (total yards per skein) = (total skeins for garment). If you are concerned about having enough yarn, buy an extra skein or two. Most yarn stores will give a credit or exchange if the leftover yarn is returned in good condition. When purchasing yarn make sure all the skeins have the same dye lot number. The same lot number means that those yarns are from the same dye batch. Colors do vary from lot to lot, so this is an important thing to remember. As for quality, almost all yarns come in better or lesser grades; they are graded according to a fiber's length, softness, and strength. Since labels don't show these grades, experience, price, or advice from a reputable yarn shop are the best guidelines for determining quality. In an animal's fleece, the best wool usually comes from the shoulders, with the quality decreasing toward the hindquarters. Because the wool in lesser grades is shorter, coarser, and less strong, the resulting yarn won't keep its shape as well; it scratches and pills more, does not last as long, and does not have as fine a luster and feel. Cottons and synthetics also come in grades. If you pull a single fiber from a lesser quality yarn, you will find that it is short and fuzzy; by comparison, a better fiber is longer, stronger, and well defined. And, finally, there are the dyes. The best ones do not run and do fade less. Better yarns, with their finer dyes, seem to glow from within; the quality of the color is richer and deeper. Purchase the best yarn that you can afford. In the long run the garment will not only look, fit, and wear better, but you will find better yarns much more pleasing to work with.

About Blocking and Maintenance

If a garment is worked at a medium tension so that the fabric and seams lie flat and even, and if the finished piece is the right size, simply shaped garments won't require any steaming or blocking. None of the garments in this book have been steamed or blocked. However, if it is necessary to make adjustments, this is how you do it. Steaming is done to smooth the fabric and seams. To start, turn the garment inside out and place it on a flat, padded surface (a couple of bath towels over newspapers or over a plastic sheet will do). Then place a thin damp cloth over the garment and *skim* a steam iron *lightly* over the surface. *Never press down*—pressure flattens the stitches and the yarn: let the steam do all the work. Leave the garment to dry in place. Blocking straightens misshapen fabrics and can alter the dimensions. In Modular Crochet blocking is done after the garment is completed. To block, immerse the piece in water, then follow the laundering instructions. As far as maintenance is concerned, the label on the yarn should tell you what to do. Most synthetics are machine washable; some yarns must be dry cleaned. Never put wool in hot water, a washing machine, or a dryer; heat will damage the yarn and cause the garment to shrink. The kindest and best treatment for most natural fibers is to wash the garment in a mild soap solution specifically designed for delicate fibers. To do this, fill a pan or sink with soap and cool water. Immerse the garment and gently squeeze the suds through the fabric; never twist, wring, or lift parts of the garment out of the water because the weight of the water will stretch the fabric out of shape. Next, rinse it thoroughly and then gently squeeze out the excess water. Let it sit in the sink for a few minutes to let the extra water run off. Gather the garment into a ball and place it in the middle of a bath towel, spread it out, then roll it up in the towel and let it sit for a few minutes. The idea is to remove as much water as possible so the fabric won't stretch, will be easy to handle when shaping, and will dry more quickly. Now place the garment in the center of another dry towel and ease it out to fit the desired measurements, keeping the shape square and the edges even. Let it dry in place. For quicker drying, change the towel when it gets wet. Keep the garment away from the heat and out of the sunlight. If the garment starts to shrink as it is drying, pin it into place with T-pins placed at a slant along the edges so it will dry to size. Never hang a crocheted garment: it will stretch out of shape; always store it folded. Pilling is caused by friction—your arm or some other object brushing across the surface of a fabric works the individual fibers loose and rolls them up into little balls—but careful brushing will remove the pills.

Yarn Suppliers List

Upon request the following
suppliers will send you
the names
of the nearest retail outlets
in your vicinity.

Belding Lily Co.
P.O. Box 88
Shelby, N.C. 28150
3 Cut Cotton Chenille
6 Cut Cotton Chenille
Sugar 'n Cream

Brunswick Yarns
230 5th Avenue
New York, N.Y. 10001
Natural Irish Wool

Bucilla
230 5th Avenue
New York, N.Y. 10001
Melody
Blue Label Cotton

Candide
100 Main Street
Woodbury, Conn. 06798
Lightweight Wool

Emile Bernat & Sons Co.
Depot and Mendon Streets
Uxbridge, Mass. 01569
Catkin, Blarneyspun

Folklorico
P.O. Box 625
Palo Alto, Calif. 94302
El Molino Rayon Floss

Joseph Galler
149 5th Avenue
New York, N.Y. 10010
Parisian Cotton
Belangor Angora

Merino Wool Co.
1140 Broadway
New York, N.Y. 10001
Naturelle

Paternayan Bros. Inc.
312 East 95th Street
New York, N.Y. 10028
Knitting Worsted

Plymouth Yarn Co.
P.O. Box 28
500 Lafayette Street
Bristol, Pa. 19007
3 Ply Indiecita Alpaca
Andes Alpaca

Reynolds Yarns Inc.
15 Oser Avenue
Hauppauge, N.Y. 11787
Icelandic Homespun,
No. 1 Mohair, Classique,
Versaille Shetland Wool,
Cotillion, Velourette,
Feu D'Artifice, Lopi,
Gleneagle Fingering Wool

Stanley Berroco Inc.
140 Mendon Street
Uxbridge, Mass. 01569
Mirabella, Dji Dji Brushed Wool

Tahki Imports Ltd.
62 Madison Street
Hackensack, N.J. 07601
Handspun Colombian Wool
Hvywght Irish Donegal Wool
Super Heavy Donegal Tweed

Ulltex Inc.
P.O. Box 918
59 Demond Avenue
N. Adams, Mass. 01247
Alpacka, Roma

William Unger & Co., Inc.
230 5th Avenue
New York, N.Y. 10001
Scheepjes Natuurwol
Arianne